THE
SHARP
SOLUTION

THE SHARP SOLUTION

A BRAIN-BASED APPROACH FOR OPTIMAL PERFORMANCE

HEIDI HANNA

WILEY

John Wiley & Sons, Inc.

Published by John Wiley & Sons, Inc., Hoboken, New Jersey.

Published simultaneously in Canada.

Library of Congress Cataloging-in-Publication Data:
Hanna, Heidi, 1974-
  The sharp solution: a brain-based approach for optimal performance/Heidi Hanna.
    p. cm.
  Includes index.
  ISBN 978-1-118-45739-9 (pbk.); ISBN 978-1-118-50669-1 (ebk);
  ISBN 978-1-118-50668-4 (ebk); ISBN 978-1-118-50661-5 (ebk)
  1. Achievement motivation. 2. Brain. I. Title.
  BF503.H366 2013
  158–dc23

                                                          2012030193

Printed in the United States of America.

10 9 8 7 6 5 4 3 2 1

SHARP: Having an edge; precise, extremely clever or astute; keen, intelligent, sensitive, alert; having a penetrating quality; observant, incisive, vigorous, active.

In memory of Amy.

Contents

Foreword   Dr. Daniel L. Kirsch   ix

Introduction   xi

1 Understand Your Operating System   1

2 Balance Your Brain   39

3 Engage Your Heart   67

4 Focus Your Mind   85

5 Energize Your Body   113

6 Strengthen Your Community   143

7 The SHARP Solution Plan   159

Final Thoughts   171

Notes   173

For More Information   181

Index   185

Foreword

The SHARP Solution is a well-written, science-based approach to incorporating sustainable behavior change to reduce stress and increase overall wellbeing. Dr. Hanna guides you through designing a personal action plan to decrease your daily stress and live a longer, healthier life. The book provides an inside-out perspective of how the body functions on a physiological and psychological level when under stress. The focus is on building resilience through mindfulness, meditation, balanced nutrition, and dedicated relaxation time.

The book is organized into five phases: brain, heart, mind, body, and community. The focus is not on *what* you should be doing to relieve your stress and be healthier, but *how* to take the knowledge that most of us have heard repeated throughout our lives, and actually make small sustainable changes to maintain a healthy lifestyle. Dr. Hanna emphasizes nutrition, physical activity, rest, and most importantly cognitive fitness. The book guides you through various aspects of brain training through her SHARP Brain Recharge technique.

The process is simple by design. It offers a variety of short, effective methods to help you shift out of a stress response into the relaxation response in just a few moments. Dr. Hanna provides a toolbox of simple techniques that you can practice and incorporate into your busy life without adding more stress and strain as you struggle to find time to relax. Through this book, Dr. Hanna represents the essence of our mission at The

American Institute of Stress—to provide evidence-based information and simple-to-follow techniques to reduce stress and improve your quality of life.

Dr. Daniel L. Kirsch, President,
The American Institute of Stress

Introduction

For most of my life, I thought I had a broken brain. By the age of 12, I had already been diagnosed with my first stress ulcer and experienced my first panic attack. It was well understood by scientists and doctors at the time that the brain was hardwired from an early age-that our mental maps had been secured soon after adolescence and could not be changed. So I accepted the fact that I would need to learn to *manage* my broken brain and try to control the symptoms, without any hope of fully healing.

A few years ago while writing my dissertation on stress and weight management, I began to learn a great deal about how the brain works. (I also learned that stress leads to weight gain, as I put on 10 pounds without changing my diet or exercise habits—but that's fodder for another book). I was burning out, completely exhausted from traveling across the globe for work. After being hospitalized with severe fatigue and crippling panic attacks, I was unsure of how I would ever return to a normal life. My greatest fears—those that cause the biggest spikes in my anxiety—are flying and public speaking; so I definitely didn't make the best choice for a career path if I wanted to live conservatively. I had pushed myself to the limit and wasn't taking care of my personal energy the way I knew I should—and my brain let me know it.

Around this time I also found out that a third grandparent of mine had been diagnosed with Alzheimer's disease. This prompted me to begin a deep dive into research to see if there was any way to try to prevent such a fate for myself or my other family members—and what I discovered changed my life. I found out that not only were there things we could do to possibly delay the development of symptoms caused by Alzheimer's disease and natural cognitive decline, but also that they were the same things that were being recommended to reshape and rewire the brain for optimal functioning. Simply put, the things that can help you have a better brain today will help you have a better brain tomorrow. Of course, it made perfect sense, but why hadn't I heard about this before?

Thanks to advances in technology that took place about two decades ago, scientists have discovered that the brain isn't actually "hardwired" after all. Pioneering neuroscientists demonstrated that through the right type of training, people could relearn abilities they'd lost through severe brain damage, with different parts of the brain taking on new roles in the operation of the body. This discovery, known as neuroplasticity, means that the brain is radically adaptable when given the right stimulus, and allotted an adequate amount of recovery.

The existence of neuroplasticity doesn't just mean that we can *heal* the brain. It also means that we can potentially *rewire* existing mental maps—which are the connections between brain cells—so that they function in a way that best serves us, thereby leading to optimal health, happiness, and performance. I have undertaken this process myself, and implemented strategies in my own routine to make sure that my brain and body support me in the midst of challenging circumstances so that I can continue doing the work I love without burning out or breaking down. While I won't introduce any new or particularly groundbreaking concepts, we *will* walk through them in a systematic way that is designed to give you maximum benefit with minimum investment. This will help you build a toolbox of strategies to boost your brainpower—strategies that won't require a great deal of your time or energy.

One of this book's key premises is that the brain tends to pull us away from anything that might be new or challenging to our system when it becomes overwhelmed. Therefore, giving you a lengthy list of requirements would completely defeat my purpose. You will not see exercises that demand pages of explanations, software programs to buy, or supplements to take. While some of these might be helpful, you can't possibly do everything that *might* be helpful for you—if you did, you'd have a new full-time job!

The important thing to remember is that very small changes, those upon which the brain can tolerate spending energy, can slowly rewire and retrain the connections in your brain to improve your operating system. It's critical that we move one small step at a time to make these changes significant, not superficial. I wrote this book to share with you the most efficient and effective ways to train—or retrain—your brain to energize your life, even if you have the busiest of schedules.

There are many excellent books documenting the science of neuroplasticity, and I have listed some of my favorites in this book's resources section. I will share some of the most exciting studies with you throughout our discussions, and I encourage you to explore the recommended texts if you are interested in reading more about the details and fascinating discoveries. My goal here is not to overwhelm your brain with more data, but rather to provide you with some very simple tactics you can use daily to bring the power of neuroplasticity into your life and create a better brain both today and for your future.

The SHARP Solution

This new understanding of how the brain works clearly shows us that taking on too much at one time is perceived as a neurological threat. It consequently causes the brain to lead us away from new supportive habits and back into old ones. Therefore, once you create a healthy, energized brain, you provide the necessary foundation for resilience and sustainable change.

The SHARP Solution provides a brain-based approach to realistic, sustainable behavior change that supports a healthier brain and, as a result, a healthier, happier body. This includes a step-by-step process in which you'll design a personal action plan to decrease stress, balance hormones, increase energy, and improve overall health, happiness, and performance.

This book will teach you specific techniques that have been shown to help relax the body, quiet the mind, and reduce symptoms of stress imbalance, which have been proven to play a role in all of the major health concerns of today, including heart disease, diabetes, cancer, stroke, and dementia. By setting the right foundation for nutrition and physical activity efforts, you also enable the body to reduce unnecessary weight while functioning more optimally—a nice side effect of bringing the body and brain back into balance. Considering the fact that two-thirds of Americans are overweight or obese, and that excess fat can be toxic to both the body and the brain, sustainable weight management must be considered part of our overall health and wellness strategy.

The SHARP Solution is broken down into five phases, working from an inside-out perspective, from brain to heart, mind, body, and community.

Phase One (brain): Balance brain chemistry with strategic relaxation and recovery.

Phase Two (heart): Create a clear vision statement that incorporates passion, purpose, and motivation.

Phase Three (mind): Increase awareness, master mindfulness, and develop your ability to focus attention on the things that matter most to you.

Phase Four (body): Nourish the body and mind appropriately with nutrition that provides a consistent, high-quality fuel source; establish a routine of general physical activity to improve metabolism; and develop sleep habits that enable you to fully recover and repair.

Phase Five (community): Strengthen social support, build a sense of connection, and boost accountability by teaching the techniques you'll learn in this process to others.

Don't be surprised if you find yourself feeling more calm, optimistic, and downright joyful as a result of this program. You will have more mental clarity, be more creative, and be better able to focus your attention on the people and things that matter most to you. You will feel more physically energized throughout the day and will restore a healthy balance that includes simple, sustainable weight management.

In order to help you experience the shift towards a healthier brain and a more effective operating system, I will guide you through the process as we go through this book. By the time you finish reading, you will already have trained your brain for more optimal health and performance.

SHARP Science

As I initially prepared this manuscript, I included a few of my favorite studies that support the practical applications and guidelines in this book. I didn't want to fill the pages with an overabundance of scientific jargon, because I recognize how important it is *not* to overload your brain with unnecessary statistics and data—especially considering how much you already have on your mind! However, I still want to highlight the incredible research that has been conducted on the brain and how it works, and explain key studies in simplified language so that it's not only easy to understand, but also to apply. You can find them in SHARP Science boxes, which allow you to read some of the most recent research. In fact, all of the studies highlighted in these boxes were published during the final editing process of this book throughout the first part of 2012. This reinforces the fact that we learn more about the brain every single day—and that it's a truly marvelous adventure into one of the most amazing and complex systems known to man.

As we gain new insight into how the brain works, it's easy to see that we have only begun to scratch the surface. For example, a recent study showed that plaques and tangles in the brain once automatically associated with brain disease might actually be a normal part of the aging process. Considering the inflammation that occurs as a natural response to daily wear and tear on the brain, it seems logical that these brain disruptions or "injuries" could develop over time. It's the same as overusing a damaged muscle; if we continue to add chronic stress and pro-inflammatory factors like processed sugar, alcohol, or certain types of fat, we can speed up this natural deterioration, making the symptoms of aging much more intense and disruptive. While we can't stop the aging process from happening, we can certainly make it more enjoyable, not only adding more years to our lives but more life to our years!

I attended a neuroscience boot camp at the University of Pennsylvania last year. At the end of the first day, we were asked to share what our biggest takeaway had been. I answered that my attempts to learn more about the brain were actually helping me understand how little we really know. I will never forget the comment from the instructor: "If the brain were simple, we'd be too stupid to figure it out." Our operating system is indeed complicated—and what makes things even more difficult to study is the fact that each one of us is uniquely designed in many ways. Therefore, what works for one person will not necessarily work for another.

That said, I've learned something as I've continued to develop my own understanding of the human condition: as unique as we all are, there are many more similarities than differences. My "broken brain" isn't actually all that different from your brain. Most importantly I've learned that our brains can be our biggest ally *or* our worst enemy when it comes to moving us towards our most important goals.

In the chapters that follow, I will share with you the tools and techniques that I have gathered from personal experience, client stories, and experts across industries that study human behavior such as physiology, psychology, neuroscience, and sociology—or what I lovingly refer to as nutriphysioneurosociopsychology (my favorite response to give people on the plane when they ask what I do—I get some pretty interesting looks). Let the adventure begin!

Understand Your Operating System

Despite the fact that your personal energy is your most valuable resource, most of us fail to manage it efficiently. As a result we often find ourselves running on empty. More often than not, this energy shortage causes us to function in survival mode, thereby limiting our productivity and engagement while taking a toll on our health and happiness. The human operating system depends on our ability to allocate resources to give us the energy we need to meet demands. Fortunately, we are designed in such a way that we can quickly make adjustments to reduce the demands on our energy that threaten our survival. We exist today because our ancestors were able do this effectively in times of an energy shortage, such as a famine, or a spike in demand, such as a predator attack. However, the antiquated system that once served us so well in times of trouble is now actually the *source* of much of our trouble. It can lead to chronic levels of toxic stress in our system, thereby undermining our health, happiness, and performance. The good news is we can use a few techniques to re-wire our operating system and design a more effective solution to deal with the demands on our energy, which will allow us to once again thrive, even in the midst of the most challenging circumstances.

There are two primary leaders that oversee the operations of your human system: your heart and your brain. Imagine that your heart functions as the CEO of your system; it's responsible for your passion, purpose, and motivation. It navigates you towards your most important goals in life, those related to your core values and beliefs. Your brain functions as your CFO; its job is to make sure you have enough energy resources to meet demands. It is the brain's responsibility to make sure that your system doesn't take on more than it can handle, and that when demands do increase the necessary adjustments are made to compensate.

As you well know if you've spent much time in business, sometimes the CEO and CFO don't see things from the same perspective. However, this partnership is essential to the survival of the organization, because if either were left alone, we could find ourselves either running around in circles or not running at all. On the one hand, the CEO is typically more emotionally driven and inspired by the big picture, and feels incredible passion to lead the organization toward its ultimate mission. Perhaps this is one of the barriers for entrepreneurs who try to take on too many roles; it's hard to be conservative about spending and investing when the passion of your heart is leading you.

On the other hand, the analytically natured CFO keeps a laser focus on resources and can often appear overly conservative and cautious, seeming distant from the heart of the organization. Sometimes this feels restricting to the CEO and slows down the growth process. Without a clear strategy in place, the CEO might chase after every inspirational idea that came its way; and conversely, the CFO could conserve resources too vigilantly, keeping the system from doing anything at all. But by working together, the CEO motivates and the CFO regulates, allowing them to meet their goals without running out of steam.

Thankfully, our CFO brain is wired to protect our energy reserves. It's constantly monitoring situations to make sure that we have the resources we need to keep the system operating.

While it is the CEO's job to get the engine running, it is the CFO's responsibility to make sure that engine *keeps* going over time. And if the human system runs out of resources, we don't get a chance to declare bankruptcy; it's lights out, for good.

Without our key energy resources, oxygen and glucose, our cells cannot generate the energy we need. Our bodies literally begin to shut down—which is what we see happen physically during a heart attack or stroke or mentally with fatigue and burnout. Knowing all of this, our CFO keeps a close watch on the balance between the energy we have and the energy we need. It communicates constantly with the body's many systems, which report back via hormones to let the CFO know how well they are operating and the status of their energy demands at any given time.

Unfortunately, sometimes the CEO and CFO have competing interests. This often happens when you know what you *should* be doing but yet can't seem to find a way to do it. Your heart may believe that a new behavior—such as eating healthier or exercising more—would be of great benefit to your system. However, your brain might recognize that both of those strategies limit the amount of energy you have available at the present moment and talk you out of it—especially if you're operating on an empty tank.

Do you ever notice how tough it is to make good decisions at the end of the day? That's because the energy that fuels your brain to think, make judgments, evaluate options, monitor your attention, and multitask is put to use all day long. So expending all of this energy making decisions at work and then trying to make a healthy choice might compromise a major energy investment. In other words, your brain will be quick to talk you out of the salad and grilled chicken and *into* a hamburger, fries, and chocolate shake.

SHARP Science: Is Obesity All in Your Head?

Scientists at the University of Turku and Aalto University, both in Finland, have found new evidence for the role of the brain in obesity. Researchers determined that the reward system in obese individuals' brains responded more vigorously to pictures of foods, whereas responses in the frontal cortical regions involved in cognitive control were dampened. Their results suggest that obese individuals' brains may constantly generate signals that promote eating, even when the body *doesn't require* additional energy.[1]

I was sitting in a hotel lounge just the other night when I overheard a very common conversation between two guests who were enjoying the free dessert buffet. Carrying a plate with a piece of pie, the woman said, "I'm on Weight Watchers and I'm counting points, but I'm starting tomorrow." If I only had a nickel for every time I've heard that statement! No matter how much you *want* to make healthy choices, when you're running on empty at the end of the day, you have no energy to support necessary willpower. Your brain convinces you that you'll *start tomorrow* because your energy will be replenished and discipline will be easier to fuel.

When we reach for poor sources of energy, we must evaluate the behavior's desired outcome and determine if there are other, more beneficial ways to get there. For example, when physical energy levels are low and you have the option to either eat a Big Mac or go for a run, your energy-hungry brain will make the obvious choice: invest, don't spend. You'll therefore find yourself drawn to the food as a smarter energy investment.

Even knowing that exercise will make you feel better in the long term isn't enough if you're running on fumes at the end—or even in the middle—of the day. You may be better off looking for another energy investment strategy in this case, such as watching a funny video, connecting with a good friend, or utilizing the Brain Recharge process we'll be discussing later in this book. These investments in your personal energy can help get you back on track without putting you into conservation mode, and ultimately fuel your progress towards your goals.

Anytime we ask the brain to help us change, it's not as simple as pleading the case that something needs to be done simply because we want to do it. We have to *prove* to the brain that the energy we need to make the change is worth the cost. If we demand too much of the brain at once, it may let you try something out for a few days; however, you'll soon find yourself returning to old habits that have been ingrained over time, and therefore require less effort and a much smaller energy investment.

Many of my high-achieving perfectionist "type-A" clients, tend to find themselves in this situation, trapped in an all-or-nothing mentality. Feeling a strong motivation to change, their minds can quickly drift back to the way things used to be. I was speaking to a large group of financial advisors when I met a former football player from my alma mater. He told me he was feeling like garbage about letting the business wear him down, so he was going to get back to his playing weight once again by incorporating the strategies I had mentioned in my talk.

I quickly asked him to tell me about his life back then to find out exactly what he'd be returning to. His days were filled with classes (when he felt like going), a steady social life, and a few hours in the gym. He loved his life, was in fabulous shape, and felt energized all the time. Then I asked what his life was like now. He told me that he'd spend up to 16 hours in the office or meeting with clients and prospects, had a young family who wanted his full attention when he got home, and was sleeping about four (mostly interrupted) hours a night. He still loved his life, but didn't feel like he had the energy to keep up with its demands.

To get back to his previous physical conditioning would require the same type of commitment, if not more due to his aging body. It was reality-check time. I asked him if he felt comfortable quitting his job, leaving his family, and moving to an island somewhere for peace and quiet. While his heart was saying, "I can do this, I've done it before, and I know how," his brain was saying, "Yeah, *right!*" Most of us have experienced our brains allowing our hearts to run away with the idea of a life change for a little while; with the right passion and purpose, we might get away with it for a few days, weeks, or even months. The CEO is in charge, and the heart has gotten the engine started. But once we've put too much strain on the system, made it feel too uncomfortable or work too hard at something, the brain will give the mind a million reasons why it needs to stop attempting to change an old habit:

- It's not actually that important.
- You can't really do it.
- You've tried and failed before so this time won't be any different.
- You're fine the way you are; heck, you're doing better than most.
- You'll start tomorrow.

The key to sustainable behavior change is to align the heart and the brain. You must get the CEO and the CFO on the same page and comfortable with the fact that you have the resources you need to change behavior just slightly, one small step at a time, without overwhelming your system. This requires a strategic plan for improving your entire system's fitness level—not just the body but also the mind.

The New Vision of Fitness

Most wellness programs of the past have focused on physical fitness in isolation, teaching strategies that quite honestly everyone already knows they *should* be doing. I've spent over a decade teaching corporate wellness courses, and I always start off asking what the group already knows about healthy living and what *they* think they should be doing to take better care of themselves. Not only do individuals know the general strategies for wellness; they are also the only experts on their own operating system. They always have an immediate answer to these questions, whether it's to eat less or more often, move more regularly, reduce stress or sleep more (just to name a few). Yet most of them are not actually *doing* any of these things. This is where the brain comes in. While nutrition, physical activity, rest, and recovery are critical for overall well-being, you must support these strategies with *cognitive* fitness—that is, the ability to use your mental energy to support your brain and body's efforts to sustain behavior. Training the brain to be fit requires both strategic exercises that are geared to challenge and develop cognitive functions, as well as strategic rest for optimal repair and recovery.

It's clear that non-stop strenuous exercise is not the best approach to being strong, coordinated, and healthy. We require regular periods of rest and recovery at all levels of biological dynamics in order for our muscles to develop and function optimally. This regular shifting between exercise and rest—called *oscillation*—is especially important when it comes to your mental energy, both as something to understand and also to regularly practice.

SHARP Science: Need To Create? Meditate.

Have you ever noticed that the harder you *try* to solve a problem, the tougher it becomes? Sometimes the best solution is to not try at all. A recent study showed that open monitoring meditation, where the individual is receptive to all the thoughts and sensations experienced, *without* focusing attention in a particular direction, increased divergent (*outside-of-the-box*) thinking, and generated more new ideas than before meditation. In contrast, focused attention meditation—trying to concentrate on something specific rather than free flowing— had no significant effect on the ability to resolve a problem. While focused attention training may help strengthen our ability to *focus*, relaxation techniques that are geared more towards non-judgmental awareness create more opportunities for insight, thereby building mental flexibility and boosting creative thinking.[2]

Science has clearly documented that it's critical to *not* over-train your brain. Instead, you need to train deliberately in ways that will actively reduce stress, encourage neural expansion, and help your brain regularly recover and express its full potential. It's important to remember that physical and mental fitness aren't just about brute strength. Yes, you do need to keep your brain fit for bouts of long hours while you deal with a mass of detail; that's part of work. But there are three distinct dimensions to mental fitness: strength, flexibility, and endurance.

To nurture these three intertwined brain qualities, you sometimes need to actively engage your mind in cognitive workouts. However, you also need to shift into recovery mode for creative insight from time to time. And at work, just like at home, you also need to be able to instantly shift into interpersonal empathy mode, so that you can relate to your team or clients at highly successful levels.

There's no way of getting around the blunt fact that work usually generates mental stress, and a stressed-out brain performs at progressively lower levels. Too much stress is without question the number-one killer of both efficiency and creativity. This is why it's vital to learn specific ways to regularly shift your focus of attention out of stress mode and into rest mode at work, thereby giving your chronically deep-fried synapses at least a few time-out moments during the day to regroup, recover, and recharge.

Some people might initially react negatively to the idea of having to set aside regular downtime for their brain. Chances are you're already feeling pressured by deadlines, and taking time off seems to be the last way to help you get things done. But just the opposite will prove to be the case. Consider the concept of muscle fatigue; without short breaks from physical stress, your muscles at some point will begin to spasm and malfunction. Periodic rest is required for the system to repair and become stronger.

Medical studies show us that the same basic thing happens in your brain. You begin to lose the mental power necessary to hold your focus on your work, which causes more errors and diminishes creative vitality. Focus is what work is all about. Your attention, like your energy, is one of the most valuable resources you possess. It's crucial to think deeply about how you are using and managing that resource by considering the following questions:

- What are you spending your energy on, or *paying* attention to?
- Are you saving any reserves?
- Do you have a long-term investment strategy to make sure that you don't run out?

Your mental capacity (strength, flexibility, endurance) drives not only performance, but also your engagement with people who matter to you. And if you don't take care of your mental fitness and stay balanced and charged for action, you can't possibly take care of anyone or anything else. As the flight attendant instructs passengers before a flight, "Please put your own oxygen mask on before assisting other passengers." I'm not sure if everyone realizes the importance of this statement. It's not just about being good to yourself; if you run out of oxygen you can't help save anyone else!

Making sure that you take time to keep your brain sharp is one of the primary responsibilities you have each day. You also want to preserve it, so you have energy left at the end of the day to spend with the people and things that matter most to you. This enables you to be at your best in the present moment *and*

stres

builds your brain health and cognitive reserve in order to support a better brain as you age.

You've probably already experienced ways in which stress damages cognitive health and performance. In this book we're going to consider the most effective methods for periodically shifting out of stress mode altogether in order to recover, rebalance, and recharge our mental energy. These essential breaks will make you feel better, revitalize your performance, and keep your brain resilient over time.

The Stress Story

It's important to note that stress is *not* the enemy here. In fact, stress is actually a good thing. People are often surprised to find out that one of the highest spikes in human mortality (death rates) occurs within the first six months after retirement. While we dedicate our lives to working hard at home and at work, looking forward to the day we can retire and fully enjoy some downtime, our body actually grows accustomed to functioning with this high level of stress. And our system is not designed to function in a state of all or nothing. A world without stress would not only be a shock to our usually amped-up system; it would also lead to quick deterioration because we would lose the stimulus for growth.

Stress, in its simplest definition, is *anything that causes change*. When endocrinologist Hans Selye originally coined the word *stress* in the mid-20th century, he used it to describe "the non-specific response of the body to any demand for change." Add a stressor of some sort and the recipient of that stressor has to adjust somehow.

Stress at its core is neither good, nor bad; in fact, it's often a positive thing when it comes to the human system. Consider exercise, which is clearly a stress to the body. We have an adaptive inflammatory response to the increased demand we put on our physical system. As a result of causing our heart and lungs to work harder than they're used to in an aerobic capacity, we become fitter and able to utilize oxygen more efficiently. During interval training (alternating short periods of high- and moderate-intensity exercise) we train ourselves to recover more quickly as we push to a point of discomfort, and then work to return to a more restful state. This both enhances our physical, mental, and emotional energy and significantly improves our quality of sleep, since our system becomes more effective at acquiring rest.

Flu shots offer another clear example of how stress to the body can cause us to enhance our defenses and become stronger. These small doses of influenza actually trigger the immune system to put up its guard and build a quicker and more effective method of attack should you be exposed to this flu virus in the future. What initially breaks your system down can—with the right amount of recovery and repair—ultimately make you stronger than before you started.

When you stop challenging yourself physically, fitness diminishes rather quickly. If you become sedentary, muscles atrophy, rendering themselves useless and causing your system to slow down energy production, which you'll notice as a decrease in metabolism. As much as you might think you want stress to just disappear, it's likely that the times in your life where you experienced the most growth were probably also the most stressful.

Stress is a stimulus for change, which is required for growth to occur. But stress levels can become toxic if they're too intense or persist for too long a time, and instead of building us up, we find ourselves breaking down.

New studies have linked chronic stress to the accumulation of proteins in the brain in the hippocampus, which is primarily responsible for forming, storing, and organizing memories. This is the same area where plaques and tangles usually first appear in Alzheimer's disease. It seems that acute stress—a single, passing episode—may be beneficial for brain plasticity and learning, but the continuous activation of stress pathways may lead to destructive pathological changes.[3]

Keep in mind that stress is different from worry. In fact two people can experience the exact same stressor and have completely different physiological responses based on how each one perceives the experience. One might see something stressful as a challenge they can overcome, while another worries about whether or not they'll be able to handle it. The body's resulting stress response is quite different in each; one person will grow stronger, while the other suffers negative consequences. And it's all based the brain's perception of the situation.

Our experience is determined by what we choose to pay attention to and how we interpret it. The point at which stress becomes toxic differs from one individual and situation to another, and everyone responds differently when they reach that breaking point. However, even while stress might be building to the point of becoming harmful, an addiction has already formed for many people, making it very uncomfortable to slow down and relax.

Taking it Easy is *Hard*

Have you ever noticed how difficult it is to actually relax? For something that's supposed to be enjoyable, slowing down can actually cause a great deal of discomfort to someone who's used to being on the go all the time. Try it right now. Close your eyes for a few moments and just try to completely relax your body and quiet your mind. See how long it takes for your brain to start wandering to your long to-do list or other worries you might be holding onto.

Without practice, relaxing is hard work!

The stress response acts on the same triggers in the brain as other addictive substances and behaviors such as drugs, alcohol, sugar, shopping, gambling, or even falling in love. Our reward system, fueled primarily by a chemical in the brain called dopamine, keeps us doing things that we perceive to be helpful for our survival.

When we repeat a behavior over and over again—such as driving the same route to work each morning—the repetition builds a habit. Add dopamine, and neural connections become even stronger, making it almost impossible to stop even the behaviors that you know are bad for you.

We all know that the things I listed above are toxic when used in excess. Despite this, when your body and brain get a hit of any of these addictive chemicals, they don't just experience the initial reward response; they begin to *crave* it once it's gone. Just like any other addiction, our tolerance level actually increases over time—even when it comes to stress. This means that we need greater amounts of stress to get the same endorphin rush, which creates a dependence that makes it increasingly uncomfortable to eliminate sources of stress.

You may consider it a strong statement to call stress an addiction; however, think about how long it takes for you to relax when you're on vacation. Or how challenging it is to keep away from email during the day even though you know it's a distraction from other things you may need to focus on. Each phone call, email, or text initiates the reward system just in anticipation of something new and potentially positive. Even though we may not enjoy what we hear on the other side, novelty in itself is something we crave.

SHARP Science: Addicted to Facebook?

According to research at the University of Bergen in Norway, the use of social media sites like Facebook has contributed to an increase in Internet addiction. Think you might be addicted to Facebook? Score yourself on the following six criteria, by responding very rarely (1), rarely (2), sometimes (3), often (4), or very often (5):

1. You spend a lot of time thinking about Facebook or planning the use of Facebook.
2. You feel an urge to use Facebook more and more.
3. You use Facebook in order to forget about personal problems.
4. You have tried to cut down on the use of Facebook without success.
5. You become restless or troubled if you are prohibited from using Facebook.
6. You use Facebook so much that it has had a negative impact on your job/studies.

(continued)

SHARP Science: Addicted to Facebook? (*Continued*)

According to the developers of the assessment, scoring "often" or "very often" on at least four of the six items may suggest a Facebook addiction. Try scheduling Facebook breaks during the day and limiting them to a specific time frame to minimize "cravings."[4]

Just today I found myself fighting the pull of the technological leash while running some errands. As I stood in line at the post office, my automatic pilot caused me to pull out my cell phone and start to check for new emails. I caught myself, chuckled a bit about the fact that I had just been writing about this very topic, and put the phone back in my bag.

Not even 20 minutes later, I had an appointment, and something that should have been relaxing turned into another work opportunity. Without even thinking about it, I sat down and immediately pulled my phone out again. And again I laughed at myself (I do a lot of that). But we all reconnect when we have downtime, right? Look around at a restaurant, or an airport, or anywhere that people have to wait; you'll seldom see them not doing anything at all. We crave busyness, and now that we have constant access to communicating and browsing and surfing, there is no reason at all not to pass the time doing *something*.

Being busy can be productive and enjoyable, so I'm not saying we should all sit around being bored all the time. But I would like you to consider that being constantly busy means being in a constant state of arousal—something that utilizes energy and quite often stimulates a chronic, underlying stress response.

The more we are "on," the more difficult it is to turn "off" when we want to, and the harder it becomes to actually relax. And relaxing is not only good for your brain—as you will soon understand, it keeps you healthy and even helps you lose weight.

Stress and Health

There are many quality studies available that clearly document how toxic stress can be to both our bodies and our brains. According to author John Medina's book *Brain Rules*, people who experience chronic stress have an elevated risk of heart attacks and strokes, decreased immune functioning, increased rates of depression, impaired sleep, poorer short- and long-term memories, and decreased cognitive performance. One study showed that adults with high stress levels performed 50 percent worse on certain cognitive tests than adults with low stress levels.[5]

If you've ever stayed up late watching TV, you've most likely seen the infomercials promising to melt away belly fat by blocking cortisol, a stress hormone that has been linked to excess fat storage, particularly around the waistline. You actually do not want to get rid of cortisol; it serves many purposes that are quite necessary for our survival. The problem with this hormone is that it triggers a metabolic response that can cause your body to store excess calories as fat. It is essentially trying to prepare the body for an emergency that is chronic in nature; or in other words, one that is not going away anytime soon.

Stress contributes to the weight gain equation in many ways, across multiple energy dimensions. Physically, it causes the body to produce a cascade of hormones that increase appetite and compel us to crave high-calorie, high-fat foods. Mentally, it prompts us to use up more of our resources—such as willpower and self-discipline—which makes the idea of sticking with a meal plan much less appealing. And when stress leads us to seek comfort emotionally, there are few things that are as effective and efficient at stimulating relaxing endorphins in our brain as comfort food.

SHARP Science: Chocolate with Breakfast?

New research from Tel Aviv University suggests that including chocolate as part of a balanced 600-calorie breakfast (including protein and carbohydrate) may help dieters lose weight and keep it off. While a reduced calorie diet can facilitate fat reduction, the brain and body can experience withdrawal-like symptoms that cause fatigue and cravings. Over the course of the 32-week-long study, participants who added dessert—cookies, cake, or chocolate—to their breakfast lost an average of 40 pounds more than a group who avoided such foods, and they kept the pounds off longer. Curbing cravings may be more important than deprivation for long-term weight loss success.[6]

Although it may seem contradictory, your brain and body love the idea of getting fatter! Consider this: Energy is your most critical resource. It fuels everything you think, feel, and do. Cells require both glucose and oxygen in order to create energy; if we run out of either, it's lights out for the entire system. Therefore, anything the body can do to conserve or preserve this natural energy source makes it more likely to survive in periods of an energy shortage.

☞ Even though most of us are not actually worried about running out of food anytime soon, the brain remains on high alert just in case. Anytime we go too long without eating, for example, this protective system is triggered. Our bodies then release hormones to help us hold on to the resources we have, and seek out more resources (calories) as soon as possible.

Let's say that you are stranded on a deserted island with no food. You don't feel hungry initially, because your stress response decreases appetite at first in order to help you focus on the other tasks you need to complete in order to survive. In time, however, adrenaline wears off; and another stress hormone called cortisol is released along with appetite increasing factors that are all designed to get you to find the most valuable (i.e., high-sugar, high-fat) food sources quickly and load up.

Remember, the brain and body love this idea, because it allows us to store more valuable glucose away for future emergencies. And as you've probably already guessed, this storage is called fat.

At the same time that we are trying to store extra energy, the brain also tries to conserve energy by slowing down metabolism. It does so by reducing the amount of fuel the body requires at that time. Only the most essential organs, emotions, and thought patterns get energy in times like these. The result? We may feel sleepy or sluggish, irritable or angry, and have a tough time concentrating.

The greater the stress, the more the brain wants to conserve energy and the more likely we are to store and protect fat in our body. This means that even if you are dieting—eating things that you believe are healthy for you in smaller portions and moving more often throughout the day—you're still going to battle against hormones that are designed to make you fat if your stress levels are high.

It's important to be aware that you can be lean but still find yourself accumulating unhealthy fat in your body and your bloodstream—both of which can be toxic to personal energy in multiple ways—without seeing a change in the scale. I have worked with many thin but stressed-out individuals who showed significantly high body-fat percentages when tested. Many of them believed they were doing everything right (dieting and exercising), when in fact they were just increasing their stress response and fat stores.

Keeping stress under control is critical to our ability to keep fat from getting out of control. In fact, you might actually get fatter if you add exercise to this already complicated equation. Now that's *really* frustrating! You could be investing precious time and energy, dragging yourself through workout after workout and actually doing more harm than good when it comes to your weight-loss efforts. Why? Because exercise is stressful to the body. When we are taking care of our needs physically, mentally, and emotionally we are able to tolerate this stress in a way that is healthy and actually makes us stronger, as a result. We have more energy, our immune system is enhanced, our heart and lungs are more effective, and so on.

However, when we aren't managing our energy effectively and we begin an exercise program when we are stressed-out or without fueling up, we might end up creating even more weight-loss resistance for ourselves as stress levels continue to skyrocket. So now instead of just thinking you are stranded without food, your brain assumes something must be chasing you. After all, our caveman and cavewoman brains can't imagine why you would exercise for fun. More stress, more fat.

SHARP Science: Forced Exercise Minimizes Positive Effects

Animal studies have shown that forced exercise may actually cause more harm than good, which may be a result of excess stress hormones hindering the body's ability to fully recover and repair. According to Mike Gleeson of the United Kingdom's Loughborough University, neither couch potato nor elite athlete is ideal when it comes to humans. Gleeson states that moderate exercise enhances the activity of natural killer (NK) cells, which are important weapons in the fight against viral infections. Stressful endurance activities such as marathons can turn down NK cell activity, leaving the body susceptible to foreign invaders. Gleeson's conclusion: "Moderate exercise has a positive effect on the immune system. So to keep colds at bay, a brisk daily walk should help—it's all about finding a happy medium."[7]

You still may find yourself losing weight, even with all this stress, but you're likely not losing *fat*. Our bodies actually utilize lean muscle protein for fuel when we go too long without eating, and we can begin losing muscle mass. It may surprise you to know that anorexic individuals—those who eat a severely low number of calories or perhaps even nothing at all—have high body-fat percentages, despite being severely underweight. This is because their lean body mass wastes away (including their heart muscle—just one deadly result of food restriction).

Therefore weight loss is not necessarily fat loss. If you're losing lean muscle, you're making it more challenging to generate energy or lose fat as your metabolism slows down, and you require even fewer calories.

This doesn't just add fat to our body; it also wreaks havoc on our brain. According to stress researcher Robert Sapolsky's groundbreaking book, *Why Zebras Don't Get Ulcers*, cortisol is so toxic to the brain that it not only hinders neurogenesis (the growth of new brain cells), it will literally kill brain cells on contact.[8]

According to the American Institute of Stress, there are numerous emotional and physical disorders that have been linked to stress, including depression, anxiety, heart attacks, stroke, hypertension, immune system disturbances that increase susceptibility of infections, and autoimmune diseases such as rheumatoid arthritis and multiple sclerosis. In addition, stress can have direct effects on the skin and gastrointestinal system, and can contribute to insomnia and degenerative neurological disorders such as Parkinson's and Alzheimer's disease. It's actually somewhat difficult to come up with any sort of disease or disorder that *isn't* caused by or at least aggravated by a stress imbalance. In fact, medical experts suggest that up to 90 percent of doctor visits are stress-related!

The key to sustainable wellness is finding a healthy balance; one in which the stress in your life is simply a stimulus for growth and change, and you can keep your hormone levels in harmony. This happens when you create balance between two complimentary systems in the body: the stress response and the relaxation response. Ideally, these systems are designed to work in partnership, so that you can tolerate stress in a healthy way. Unfortunately, most of us become so overwhelmed with stress on a daily basis we fail to make relaxation a priority. As a result, our systems are out of whack and our mental energy is in a constant deficit.

Boost Your Brainpower

Just like the rest of our body, the brain works in a way optimally suited for our biological survival. Because we require constant energy to fuel our cells, and because our natural energy supply is limited, our control center is designed to expend as little energy as possible. This made perfect sense in times gone by; however, the problem today is that our ancient automatic-pilot mode, originally designed to help us survive in more primitive settings, actually keeps us from maintaining a healthy lifestyle.

According to cognitive scientists, we have two very different processing systems in the brain that are always vying for dominance. There's the ancient automated system (or *auto-brain*), and the newer reflective system (or *thinking brain*). In times of danger, the automated system takes over and allows us to act quickly, which is important when we need to react to a threat or run away from danger. "Don't think, just do."

For raw survival purposes, our auto-brain has to be ready to take charge at any moment. Even in contemporary times, there are sudden dangerous occasions when taking time to think through or debate multiple choices could leave us dead in our tracks, such as a truck barreling right at us on the road or a fire rapidly burning in our home. Times like these call for an immediate response, a preprogrammed knee-jerk reaction to a situation.

However, the thinking mind takes over when we're faced with choices requiring reflection, and uses whatever time is needed to make the best decision for the situation. This part of the brain is especially important when we try to think outside the box to be creative, when we work to manage interpersonal relationships, and when we attempt to make choices that go against what our natural survival instincts might want us to do, such as punch someone who is aggravating us or push someone out of our way when waiting in line. Learning, judgment, evaluating, storing memories, and emotional regulation are all part of the reflective system.

It can be helpful to have a general awareness of the brain's different sections and their primary responsibilities in order to see how they work together—and sometimes get out of touch. Many neuroscientists and educators use the "hand model" of the brain to help people develop a basic understanding of the brain's structure and how it works.

If you look at the base of your hand, where the wrist connects with your forearm, you can imagine the brain stem connecting to the spinal cord. At the base of the human brain in the cerebellum and brain stem is the spot that controls our most basic instincts and regulates our automatic, unconscious bodily functions. This is often referred to as our reptilian or *lizard brain*, as it's an element of the brain that we share with almost all animals on the planet.

Extend your thumb across the palm of your hand and you will see where your limbic system is located, and where you would find your mammalian *monkey brain*. This area controls our more complex functions related to emotional reactions. Most mammals lead with their monkey brain, which fuels the basic responses to fear and desire.

Wrap your fingers over your thumb and you will see a representation of the cerebral cortex, the outer layer of brain tissue surrounding the monkey brain, called the forebrain and the frontal lobes. This cognitive area allows for logical, emotionless thought such as deductive reasoning and delayed gratification.

The mind's automated function predates its thinking function by many millions of years. In fact, it's often called the *lizard brain* to differentiate it from the newly evolved, rational section of the human brain that's capable of complex analytical thought. Using our unique human brain lets us think through and determine our responses to a situation rather than just instinctively reacting. When we are faced with sudden threats to our system, we often don't have time to stop and analyze what's going on. These are the times we're lucky to have our lizard and monkey brains to quickly get us to safety, employing our reflexive fight-or-flight response.

But usually, we do best when we consciously observe our habitual lizard and monkey reactions to situations and learn how to change our programming when those reactions don't benefit us. And other than an emergency, the quickest way to shift into automatic-pilot mode is to spread our mental energy too thin by taking on multiple tasks at the same time.

Avoid Multitasking Disasters

One of the key insights to come recently from cognitive science tells us that when we multitask, we tend to drop out of high-level rational decision-making, and slip into monkey-brain reactions in our various split activities. Because we have so many things going on, we operate mostly on automatic pilot, rather than reflecting on our decisions and actions. Multitasking often prompts us to make mindless decisions that may end up causing serious problems with important responsibilities or relationships.

The next time you find yourself trying to do a million things at once and getting irritable with someone you care about, remind yourself that you're using your monkey brain, and work on acting more like a rational human being. Give each moment your full attention, so that you respond in a more thoughtful, beneficial way. You may also consider trying something I've done with a few close friends: When someone seems distracted, ask them if they're using their "monkey brain" (use this method at your own risk).

Of course, most of us have trained our brains to operate in multitask-mode the majority of time due to our fast-paced, need-it-yesterday society. And although we have made it easier to multitask, that doesn't mean we should do it. No matter how gifted you believe you are at doing 10 things at once, there are well-documented studies suggesting that multitasking not only decreases performance; it also stresses the brain unnecessarily. Yet the brain will continue to prefer to lead you in this direction because of its resource-management focus. In other words, even though it takes energy to multitask, it takes even *more* energy to try to change a bad habit. And the rush of needing to get things done quickly feeds our stress addiction by neuro-chemically rewarding us for bad behavior.

That said, by expending some time, energy, and a little bit of patience, you *can* rewire your brain to prefer a more single-minded focus. It will just require some practice; and you'll need to take small steps so that you don't overwhelm your system by changing too much at once.

There are two reasons why this single-focus concept is critical to our brain-training program. First, we should remember that many of our judgments, decisions, and actions do not emerge from a place of thoughtful consideration or mindfulness. Too often, we are simply creatures of habit. We react to a situation or a person based on previous prejudice and programming, or our lizard-brain fight or flight reflexes, rather than relating consciously using whole-brain intelligence and wisdom.

Unfortunately, this is where a lot of our prejudices and biases can show their ugly heads. Someone who has struggled with a particular group, such as a political party or religious affiliation, makes assumptions based only on previous interactions. This is aggravated if the person from the past posed a threat to one's viewpoint or challenged someone to the point of discomfort. Survival instincts would lead us away from interacting with people who threaten our sense of self, even when it's the best thing for our personal development (and this can be a big problem when organizations lack diversity).

Second, and most important, when our past programming is less than desirable, we possess the inner ability to train our auto-brain to respond differently. Thanks to neuroplasticity, we can repeatedly focus our attention in particular directions that stimulate our brains to create new pathways or expand old ones. This allows us to learn new and improved mental and behavioral patterns.

SHARP Science: Meditation Builds Mental Muscle

Over the past decade, there has been significant evidence of meditation shaping the structure of the brain through neuroplasticity—and more is being discovered every day. A recent report by UCLA researchers suggests that long-term meditators have larger amounts of gyrification, or folding of the cortex, which may allow the brain to process information faster than people who do not meditate. Researchers noticed a direct correlation between the amount of gyrification and the number of meditation years, providing further proof of the brain's ability to adapt to environmental changes over time.[9]

There are many examples of this core re-training process in sports and other types of competition. Skilled chess players and elite athletes have taught themselves to analyze complex situations more quickly in order to respond in the best way, as fast as possible. Through practice, these superstars are able to consciously train elements of their brain that would normally be part of the reflective, thoughtful system to happen automatically, without much time or energy. And it's not all that different for non-elite athletes. I had practiced softball for 13 years by the time I was in college, so many of my abilities had been ingrained into my operating system and therefore required very little thought to execute. Sometimes they were survival-based efforts, such as flipping my glove up immediately to protect my forehead from a fastball being returned in my direction. Other times, they were part of a strategic plan that we had trained so frequently that it did not require any time to pause, reflect, and make a good choice. If a slow ground ball came at me with a runner on third who seemed a bit further from the base than she should be I instantly knew to fake the throw to first and then turn to surprise the runner on third with a quick toss to get her out (I loved the fake-out play).

Even simple parts of our daily routines are loaded with examples of the auto-brain in action. Think of all of the things you do during the day that you could almost do in your sleep (and maybe sometimes do). You get up and turn the coffee pot on, brush your teeth, take a shower, get dressed, drive to work, and walk to your office. Did you really have to make a conscious effort to do all of that?

Because our auto-brain requires a very small amount of energy compared to rational decision-making, it's always going to be the preferred way of perceiving a situation, processing information, and facilitating behavior. Our auto-brain is certainly not a bad thing. It's actually a most marvelous phenomenon, as long as we remain aware of how it functions, so that we can be sure it's moving us in the right direction. Remaining aware in the present moment is crucial to ensuring that your automated functions and reflex habits actually assist instead of hinder you.

Even when we're not very conscious of what's happening around us, our brain assesses situations constantly, often making accurate associative and habitual interpretations. And the auto-brain tends to see what it expects to.

Below, you'll find a good example of how your auto-brain works. Read through the following paragraph and see how much you understand:

"According to a research study at Cmabridge University, it deosn't mttaer in what order the ltteers in a word are, the only iprmoetnt thing is that the frist and lsat ltteer be in the rghit pclae. The rset can be a total mses and you can still raed it wouthit porbelms. Tihs is bcuseae the human mind does not raed ervey lteter by istlef, but the word as a wlohe."

People are often surprised by how easily they can read this paragraph. Because our brain focuses primarily on patterns and is able to make assumptions, even gibberish can make sense as long as certain patterns remain consistent (which, in this case, means the first and last letters are accurate).

Remember: Your brain wants to conserve energy for possible threats during the day. Therefore, it prefers to use automatic pilot mode as often as possible. Habits save us a great amount of mental energy. In *The Power of Full Engagement*, co-authors Jim Loehr and Tony Schwartz propose that up to 95 percent of human behavior happens while we're in this automated state of mind, while only about 5 percent is conscious, self-regulated behavior.[10]

We call these mostly automated activities our *habits*. They enable us to get much more done during the day than would be possible if we had to concentrate our full conscious attention on tasks like tying our shoes and brushing our teeth. Habits are patterns of thought and behavior that we've performed so often and so successfully that they become programmed into our auto-minds and no longer require our full attention.

Habits - psychology

Changing Pathways: Improving Habits

The ability to develop new habits is one of the primary survival strategies of living organisms. Unfortunately, we can become conditioned with bad habits (ones that undermine a healthy, fulfilling life) just as easily as the good ones. And those stubborn bad habits are very difficult to change, because we fall into them automatically after years of using them—whether we were trying intentionally or not.

Everything we think or do in life, whether positive or negative, has a training effect and, if done often enough, establishes a new habitual pattern. If you find yourself grabbing fast food on a regular basis, you will soon feel pulled in that direction when you start to get hungry. Stay up late several nights working (or writing a book), and you will train your brain to see this as the norm, making falling asleep at a decent hour much more challenging. If you sit at your desk too much and don't get up and go outside for regular exercise, you're reinforcing yet another unhealthy habit.

Repetition is the primary act of training. Anything you do often enough becomes a habit. For instance, if you fixate on negative worried thinking, you're going to develop a mental habit and may find yourself stuck dwelling on what's bad in life instead of noticing what's good. And unless you consciously make an effort to change a bad habit, your brain will keep these pathways well-paved as you automatically continue using them. Fortunately, the brain-training principles I introduce in this book will show you how to consciously change your mental energy's focus. You'll learn to develop more supportive habits that are less draining and thus easier to maintain. Because we have such an amazing operating system that can help us auto-mate important processes in our lives, we can choose to actively train our brains to move us regularly in the right direction—and thus make our auto-brains truly serve us.

Note that your power to change habits depends on where you choose to focus your attention during each moment of the day. In fact, your habits of attention can be seen as the bedrock of all your habits. You'll likely notice that most of the time, you aren't taking conscious control of where you focus your attention. It's operating on automatic pilot.

Any and all cognitive training requires that you *consciously decide* to concentrate on particular directions that serve you well; that's what brain-based training is all about. You shift your attention in a new or valued direction, and continue to hold your focus in that direction while you perform certain mental actions, or while you observe certain natural happenings, such as your breathing. During this process of disciplined focused attention, time and repetition will lead you to develop a new habit designed specifically to improve your life. With your heart and brain in alignment regarding your motivation and available energy resources throughout the day, sustainable change becomes possible.

The Training Plan: Hitting the Target

In order to build a brain-training program that will support healthy behavior change, it's important that we utilize a proven change process, one that provides the inspiration, information, and implementation that you can incorporate into a busy routine. To do this, we will move through the five-phase approach outlined in the introduction, which consists of balancing the brain, engaging the heart, focusing the mind, energizing the body, and building a supportive community. Each phase can be seen as a ring of a bull's-eye, with the sweet spot being the intersection where all five elements are working together in harmony.

At our core is the need to balance the brain, the controller of our resources, by providing a sense of security. Safety is our brain's key mission; it wants to keep our system fueled appropriately for each situation so that we can sustain life. Without a sense of safety, our entire operating system functions out of sync, so creating a balanced brain is the first phase of *The SHARP Solution*.

The second phase incorporates the energy of our heart— our spirit—fueled by our passions, values, and motivation. Driven by our sense of purpose, we can then incorporate phase three, our mental energy, to focus our attention in the directions that are most important to us.

Moving out to phase four, we come to our physical energy, and our need for nourishment, movement, and sleep. Finally, a healthy environment and strong sense of community provide us with the accountability and support we need to continue on our journey over time.

In the chapters that follow, we will walk through *The SHARP Solution*'s five phases of brain-based training that create a high-functioning operating system. After each step, you will complete a specific exercise to implement one of the core techniques. By the time you finish each chapter, you will already have applied the training process, and will be on your way to building a healthier, more fit brain that will support you in your important missions in life.

Training Exercise #1: Breathe

The first step in balancing brain chemistry is to simply turn your attention to your breathing on a regular basis because as soon as you focus your attention on your breathing, your entire respiratory system begins almost instantly to self-correct and expand, bringing more oxygen to your brain.

Breathing exercises can be a wonderful way to start your day with focus and clarity. They can also recharge you in the midst of a chaotic schedule, or help rebalance your energy physically, emotionally, mentally, and spiritually before transitioning home at the end of the day.

Focusing your attention to your breath might seem overly simplistic in the face of major stressors at work and home. However, your ability to shift your attention away—even temporarily—from stressing thoughts to the bodily experience of your inhales and exhales carries remarkable power to initiate relaxation and restore hormonal balance.

At first you may find that watching your own breathing, is in itself challenging. Most people do because this seemingly simple shift from being lost in stressful thoughts to being focused on your inner experience is in reality a great leap of the mind.

Remember that any exercise is valuable only if it's a bit of a challenge to perform at first. So give yourself a few weeks to explore the power of breath-recovery in creating a sense of calm energy.

Right now, let's jump in and begin your actual training with a simple practice:

Even while reading these words, begin to focus your mind's attention more and more on the actual sensations you're experiencing in your nose . . . in your chest . . . in your belly . . . as you breathe.

Feel the air flowing in and out of your nose as the beginning point for the recovery process . . . don't make any effort to change your breathing, just feel it. The air flowing in . . . the air flowing out . . . and now expand your awareness to also include the sensations of movement in your chest and belly as you breathe.

Continue breathing freely for another minute or so . . . and begin to notice how your breathing naturally, all on its own, begins to expand . . . to deepen . . . to become smoother . . . and more enjoyable.

Enjoy the experience of simply breathing in the present moment, and relax.

For a free, guided imagery track to help with your breathing practice, visit www.synergyprograms.com.

Balance Your Brain

stress

P hase One of *The SHARP* Solution focuses on the head honcho when it comes to energy management, the brain. By restoring brain balance with strategic relaxation and recovery, we move one step closer to an optimized operating system. I will be introducing techniques throughout this book that are aimed at helping you initiate the relaxation response. You've already experienced it in the previous chapter's training exercise; now I'd like to teach you the process and tell you why it's such a critical part of the health and wellness journey.

I've spent a lot of time describing the stress response, which is an activation of the body's sympathetic nervous system. The body's opposing system is called the *parasympathetic nervous system*, and its job is to facilitate a response that keeps our body in balance. This is a calming, relaxing process that ideally functions in harmony with the stress response in order to give us enough of a stimulus to grow while getting enough recovery to repair so that growth can actually happen.

Most of us suffer from a significantly imbalanced nervous system because we are on high alert the majority of the time. As demands on our time and energy increase, we feel pressure to do more with less and move our own self-care to the bottom of our priority list. We know it's not good for us, but we convince ourselves that we'll get to it someday. The problem is, someday never comes, unless we schedule, commit, and make it a priority.

Fortunately, the relaxation response is very simple to initiate, and can be done quite quickly. With a little bit of practice, you can employ it in the midst of even the most chaotic situations. In fact, this is how many people deal with anxiety and even panic disorders; they learn to initiate the relaxation response when feeling overwhelmed in order to change their physical and mental reactions to a given situation.

The Relaxation Response

Mind/body medicine pioneer Dr. Herbert Benson first studied the impact of the mind on the body with an animal model. Benson and his colleagues at Harvard Medical School looked at monkeys who were rewarded for controlling their blood pressure level with brainpower alone. The study's results were published in the *American Journal of Physiology* in 1971.[1]

Interestingly, Benson discovered the relaxation response in the very same room where famous Harvard physiologist Walter B. Cannon discovered the stress response. Cannon first spoke about the biological response that occurred during stress, where adrenaline and noradrenaline (also known as epinephrine and norepinephrine) were released to increase heart rate, breathing rate, blood pressure, metabolic rate, and blood flow to the muscles, preparing the body to either do battle with an opponent or flee the scene. This was described as being part of our survival-based fight-or-flight instinct, designed to protect us from danger.

Yet the relaxation response is undoubtedly even more important to use as a protection mechanism in modern times, since anxiety and tension often trigger an inappropriate stress response in the body. As a result, we don't utilize the same hormones that should be stimulating us to perform some sort of action for their intended purpose—and the impact becomes toxic to our system.

Humans are the only species, it seems, who can anticipate or perceive a threat even if it *doesn't* truly exist. Whether it's a lion storming at us in the jungle or our boss rushing through our office door, the hormonal response is the same. What we actually do with that response, however, is quite different; because although we may want to fight or flee, it's usually not an option. Benson and his colleagues initially found that there were four simple components necessary to initiate the relaxation response: a comfortable position, a quiet environment, a mental device (word, phrase, or sound repeated), and a passive attitude.

After continued research, however, they discovered that people truly only needed two of the components: a mental device and a passive attitude. Someone could actually be jogging along a busy highway and still elicit the response as long as they were able to maintain their mental focus and return to it when distracting thoughts interfered. Runners who claim to be "in the zone" may actually find the rhythmic nature of the running motion and the sounds of their steps hitting the pavement to be quite soothing, as long as they can keep their mind from wandering and getting caught up in past or future concerns.

Similarly, walkers, swimmers, cyclists, and other athletes can also find themselves getting in the zone of their physical activity and tuning out all other thoughts. If they can focus their attention on something positive, they can perform even complex tasks all while in a calm, clutch state of mind. These active forms of recovery can still help to recharge the brain just as effectively as the more passive techniques that we usually imagine when we hear the word *relaxation*.

The key to a successful recharge process is learning what works for you and creating a consistent practice that you can sustain over time. Remember that although it seems a bit contradictory, relaxing can be hard work. However, once you push through the initial discomfort of quieting your mind, your mental muscle will become stronger and more flexible, and you'll be able to tap into relaxation more quickly and effectively.

Reasons to Recharge

Your brain is a remarkable system that can perceive outside sensations, process that data, and respond intellectually, emotionally, and physically. It can use memory association to reflect upon a situation, then generate ideas and orchestrate game plans to accomplish your goals. Meanwhile, it is running your entire physiological show—from heartbeat to saline balance to muscular performance and the rest—at mostly unconscious levels. And all this requires *energy*.

When it comes to the brain's responsibilities, you are designed to spend a portion of your focus time:

- Thinking and problem solving
- Perceiving and enjoying your bodily experience
- Feeling emotions and relating
- Focusing inward toward relaxation and peace

Striking a balance is best and, in the long-term, required for your brain's performance and health. However, most of us have developed long-held habits of fixating too much on the first function in that four-part list you just read.

Think back to being in the classroom, which in many ways, is just like being in the boardroom. You were forced to sit still in one immobile position for long periods of time each day, and focus solely on *thinking*, as opposed to perceiving and feeling and enjoying movement and relaxation. This is the story of mankind for the last hundred years or so, and our habits have become deeply ingrained. We must regain a healthy balance between the brain's four primary natural functions if we're to feel better, be healthier, and have higher levels of mental performance.

We all know what it feels like to burn out. We reach that point all too often where we've temporarily exhausted our biochemical supplies of brain fuel and hormones, and just can't think straight or relate well at all.

The solution to this is to dedicate time to strategically shifting our focus away from stressor mental activities toward rejuvenation activities. It doesn't take long, and doing it regularly (at least three times a day) brings remarkable uplifts of vitality, clarity, empathy, and creativity—four of the boosts we need most in order to be successful and to enjoy life at work and at home.

SHARP Science: Meditation Makes Multitasking Manageable

Studies have shown that trying to do too many things at once can be stressful to the brain. However, meditation training prior to multitasking could make the work smoother and less stressful, according to new research from the University of Washington. Researchers recruited three groups of human resource managers for the study. The first group received Mindfulness-Based Stress Reduction (MBSR) training using meditation; the second received body relaxation training; and the third received no training. Participants were given a stressful (but quite common) test of their multitasking abilities that required them to use e-mail, calendars, instant messaging, the telephone, and word-processing tools to perform common office tasks. The meditation group reported significantly lower levels of stress than either the control or relaxation group. Once the control group received the MBSR training, their stress levels dropped to those similar to the original meditation group. Meditating before multitasking also seemed to help participants concentrate for longer periods of time. They spent more time on tasks, switched tasks less often, and took no longer to complete the overall job than the others. After the training, both the meditators and those trained in relaxation techniques showed improved memory for the tasks they were performing, while the control group did not.[2]

When we utilize relaxation strategies we are able to meet three key goals of balancing brain chemistry: recovery, rebalancing, and recharging.

1. **Recovery.** In general, most of us do not need to do *more*; we need to do less. We're over-stressed, not under-stressed. Therefore, a crucial item on our daily to-do list should be to periodically and intentionally *not do anything at all.*

   I know that spending precious time away from your to-do list feels a bit counterproductive and even scary. It seems to run contrary to the whole notion of training the brain to perform at higher levels. However, just the opposite is true. Physically, we can't expect to run constantly all day. We must take breaks and teach ourselves how to pause, rest, and recover.

To optimize our brain power, we need to create a stimulus that prompts us to adapt. However, most people over-train their brains, which leads to overuse injuries that not only slow us down, but also literally erode the brain's structure.

When we are able to recover mentally on a regular basis, we reduce the symptoms of overuse and keep our operating system strong. This provides us with the first aspect of cognitive fitness: *brain strength*.

2. **Rebalancing.** Taking time to pause and get back in tune with our natural breathing process, thereby stimulating the body and brain's relaxation response, allows our system to regain its natural state of internal balance, or *homeostasis*. Studies consistently show that we experience chronic stress, worry, confusion, and fatigue when we are out of balance, because our brain cannot operate efficiently.

If we choose to regularly regain balance by shifting our attention *away* from mental and emotional stressors and *toward* positive, present-moment physical experience, we enable our mind to return to a more harmonious state. This allows us to be more collaborative, creative, and hopeful. In this positive, balanced state, our brain can help us perform at our best and keep our operating system flexible. This is our second aspect of cognitive fitness: *brain flexibility*.

3. **Recharging.** As mentioned before, our mental energy is not a limitless resource. In order to keep our systems functioning at their best over time, we must strategically invest energy back into them. We do this by removing our attention (just temporarily) from energy-draining, problem-solving thinking and focusing on the primary charging mechanism of our body: our breathing. You have already begun to experiment with this recharge process in Chapter 1. With practice you will see that every time you tune into your breath experience, you show yourself love and support. As soon as you focus on your breathing, your mind temporarily lets go of the habitual fixations that drain you.

Instead, you focus on the oxygen intake system that directly brings new energy into your brain and body. When your breathing is short, shallow, and uneven, your entire being is caught up in that tension, thereby compromising the natural flow. You must act consciously and regularly to break this stressed-breathing habit. This is a primary brain-training challenge, and you will need to commit seriously to the brain recharge practice in order to create a new free-breath habit.

By scheduling specific recovery time throughout the day, you will increase your energy holistically—physically, mentally, emotionally, and spiritually—so that you're running on a full tank and able to be best self. A brain that is full of energy will support your health, happiness, and performance, and keep your operating system functioning optimally over time. This is the third aspect of cognitive fitness: *brain endurance*.

I recommend building a routine of a three-by-three recharge practice, starting with just 3 minutes, 3 times a day in mental recovery. I realize that spending 9 minutes a day focusing on something other than work is a lot to ask. However, *you* are your most valuable resource. If you don't take care of yourself, you can't possibly take care of anyone or anything else. And while we all know this, we often don't act like we really believe it.

The SHARP Brain Recharge Process

As we explore all the various aspects of brain training step by step throughout this book, I'll guide you in mastering one particular brain exercise that will stand at the heart of this discussion: the *SHARP Brain Recharge*. The format will appear quite simple, and that's just how we want it. The process isn't meant to make your brain do more work; that's most likely the problem in the first place. We need just the opposite—a short, effective method that enables you to temporarily shift out of work mode altogether for just a few minutes.

Why should you do this? Because your brain absolutely needs cognitive downtime in order to function optimally. You already know that just taking time out to catch your breath usually doesn't get the brain recovery job done; your mind is so used to going non-stop that it doesn't know *how* to turn off. I'll teach you my version of this cognitive-shifting technique, which I guarantee will become one of the core assets in your mental energy bank. It gets the job done fast, and provides you with a significant energy return on your time investment.

A mere three-minute SHARP Brain Recharge break fuels up to two hours of high-charge, high-performance action in its wake. That's pure gold in a professional environment where you're likely to be evaluated on your higher mental performance, social verve, innovative insight, and overall brightness of mind.

You will find that the SHARP Brain Recharge not only quiets your busy, stressed-out mind; it also makes your physical body feel good almost immediately. This in turn raises your overall mood, and boosts the energy you exude to others, so that when you return your focus to the work at hand, your overall stress is down and your health profile is up.

The underlying idea here is not to train harder, but to train smarter. The brain is similar to any muscle that you want to grow; you must use it regularly in order to maintain its conditioning. As with your biceps and hamstrings, if you're not strategic about how you train, you can find yourself constantly breaking down instead of building up.

Too much mental training leads to over-usage injuries such as fatigue, distraction, slow processing, cellular atrophy, and subtle brain damage. Giving yourself a few moments of mental recovery helps to reduce these symptoms of overuse. It also allows you to begin treating the core cause of stress and mental malfunction.

SHARP Science: Take Breaks to Control Cravings

Studies have shown that taking breaks not only enhances physical energy and mental performance; it may also decrease unhealthy food cravings. According to a study published in the journal *Appetite*, 78 regular chocolate eaters were asked to abstain from snacking on chocolate for two days. The individuals were then divided into four groups. Two groups were asked to take a brisk 15-minute walk; afterwards one returned to a difficult task, while the other was given a low-stress task. The other two groups were asked to have a rest instead of a walk prior to completing the same difficult or low-stress tasks. While the difficulty of the task made no difference in the amount of chocolate they ate, those who had done physical activity before working consumed half the amount of chocolate as the sedentary groups. In other words, while it may feel easier to reach for sugar when you need an energy boost, a brisk walk may do even more to enhance mood, focus, and attention without the extra calories.[3]

In order to be sharp, it's important that we train our brain strategically to focus our energy and attention on the people and things that matter most to us. Unfortunately, most of us tend to run ourselves into the ground with nonstop, high-speed, stressful mental activity during the day. For example, we:

- Multitask, which causes stress.
- Worry a lot, which takes loads of energy out of our available inner supply.
- Work against deadlines, which cause chronic anxiety.
- Stay in problem-solving gear without a break for too long, which strains our system.

- Get stuck in shallow, tense breathing, which reduces the flow of oxygen to our brain.
- Remain sitting for far too long, which further stresses our body and zaps our vitality.

You can avoid many of these behaviors by learning a periodic recharge program to use several times during the day. This new habit will almost instantly shift you out of stress-fatigue mode and into recovery-recharge mode. This chapter will include a short and enjoyable process where you spend just a few minutes a day turning your thinking brain off to relax, rebalance, and recharge. Remember, scheduling firm appointments to recharge your energy and sharpness needs to be a priority. Since your energy is not an unlimited resource, taking care of yourself is not an option; it's a necessity.

Because our mind is fueled by the same energy source as our body, we can often confuse demands across dimensions. For example, when your brain is tired from thinking all day long, you can easily mistake this energy deficit as a need for food. You may discover that this hunger disappears when you conduct a brain recharge and invest positive energy back into your brain. And even if this is not the case, you will at least make healthier choices when it comes to fueling your body once you've balanced your brain chemistry and decreased the cortisol often responsible for unhealthy cravings.

Consider the fact that most arguments between couples occur in the evening, when energy reserves are low. From a survival perspective, it is not critical for us to be patient, loving, and kind; instead, we tend to be irritable, angry, and aggressive. When our energy tank is empty or running on fumes, our brain will chose to fuel only the most critical of mental and physical functions—those that protect us.

Recharging throughout the day can look very different depending on the individual. One person may find that sitting in mindfulness meditation for 20 minutes does the trick. Another person might only require short-form meditation for two to three minutes. It doesn't matter whether it's spending time in your garden, cooking a healthy dinner, or taking a quick snooze. Anything you do that recharges your personal energy will be of great value as you try to invest in the people and things that matter most to you.

SHARP Science: Take a Break to Maintain Memory

New research has identified a neural mechanism that directly links repeated stress with impaired memory. Stress hormones are known to influence the pre-frontal cortex (PFC), the brain region that controls executive functions such as working memory and decision-making. Dr. Zhen Yan and colleagues at the State University of New York at Buffalo found that there was a significant loss of glutamate receptors in response to repeated stress in juvenile rats. Glutamate signaling plays a critical role in PFC function. By determining the molecular happenings, the researchers were also able to block these mechanisms to inhibit the drop in receptors and therefore prevent stress-induced memory loss. Taking a break to decrease stress hormones and increase feel-good chemicals like dopamine may hinder damage caused by stress while strengthening the neural connections that keep memory strong.[4]

You should never consider it selfish to invest in your own energy; it's actually one of the smartest ways you can give to others. After all, what you have to offer is ultimately determined by the energy that you have to give, and how can you possibly have anything to share if you don't have anything in your tank?

Pause and Relax

Meditation has become a buzzword for relaxation programs, as many quality studies have shown that meditation can quiet the mind and calm the body. Yet most people struggle when trying to develop a meditation practice; they either lack the structure or guidelines necessary to begin, or are trying to learn a challenging process too quickly.

The media has portrayed traditional meditation as being something only for gurus and their followers. While it's true that some forms of meditation are quite difficult to master and require a teacher, a new approach called short-form meditation does not. It takes only three to five minutes a session, can be learned readily, and can be included in a busy workday as a vital lifeline to refreshing mental energy and focusing attention.

The purpose of meditation is to refocus your attention in rewarding directions. In order for such a practice to be effective, it should include the following:

- A time frame set aside for the recharge experience (scheduled as a priority)
- A comfortable position (whatever feels relaxing to you)
- A somewhat quiet environment (free from distractions)

- A mental focusing device or technique (sound or word that is repeated)
- A non-judgmental attitude (you cannot be critical of yourself or your process)

Of course, there will be times when you can't escape to your man cave to meditate; however, this is no reason not to take a recharge break. You can't let your environment dictate your life. Regardless of your surroundings, you can always just close your eyes (or look at something calming in your office), focus your attention on your breathing and whole-body presence, and concentrate on a statement that will quickly shift your brain into a sensory experience that stimulates your natural sense of balance and well-being.

This chapter introduces the notion that you can use discipline to initiate the relaxing—and not just flexing—of your mental muscles. Consciously focusing on your breathing initiates a return to a smoother, more relaxed breathing process.

Ready . . . Set . . . Recharge

You've already learned the general framework of the SHARP Brain Recharge process in our first training exercise. Hopefully you're continuing to stay aware of your breathing, even while reading these words. Like any good habit, the more you do it, the better you're able to feel and perform it—and the more ingrained it becomes.

However, don't be surprised if just turning your attention to your breathing seems like a real challenge in the beginning. That's why I'm here as your coach, to help you with the initial steps of developing a new brain fitness routine and lead you through the habit-formation process successfully.

Let's look a little more closely at the five considerations for a successful recharge break, so that you have a solid sense of how to approach your new habit:

1. **Scheduling.** A habit is something that you repeat fairly regularly. You will need to discipline yourself to do this exercise three times a day if possible. This means making an effort to set aside the time and sticking with your intention.

    If you don't do this, you simply will not train the new habit, and you won't experience any gain. So, see if you're willing to dedicate nine minutes a day, right now, to a brain training exercise that provides great value. If so, take a few minutes to plug in a recharge break three times a day for the next week to get started.

    I'd highly recommend setting an alarm to remind you, and to help snap you out of work mode. I encourage you to commit to one month of doing this self-discipline process. Then, you can evaluate the results, examine the new habit, and decide if you want to sustain it long-term at the end of the month.

2. **Quiet Environment.** When you're home, it's relatively easy to regularly retreat into a quiet room, establish a standard place to sit or lie down, and move through the recharge break. When you're at work, you'll just have to make do with your situation as best you can.

    It's important *not* to be overly fussy about finding the perfect environment for your break, mainly because there's no such thing. Discipline yourself to take a break and move through the three-minute process regardless of where you are so that you can train yourself to recharge in *any* circumstance.

If you work in an office, you might want to consider explaining to your employer and fellow workers what you're doing during your three-minute breaks in order to get their understanding and support. And if your colleagues and manager see you doing this and realize how much more productive it's making you, there's a chance that your employer will make recharge breaks a voluntary company policy. After all, everyone gains when you pause and refresh!

3. **Comfortable Posture.** It is not necessary to sit in the traditional full lotus cross-legged position in order to achieve the benefits of meditation. Sitting upright in your chair at work will do fine. The most important thing is to settle into a comfortable posture, ideally with an upright spine, so that your body feels aligned and balanced.

Give yourself a few moments to move around and adjust as you focus on your breathing in this position. Don't force yourself to sit still at first. Let that stillness happen organically as you start to settle down. Your breathing will naturally move your body a bit. After all, breathing is movement.

Sit more upright as you inhale, even resettling in your chair, and then contract your belly muscles and let your chin drop as you exhale completely, allowing a wave of relaxation to flow from the top of your head to the tips of your toes.

4. **Mental Focusing Aid or Technique.** Traditional meditation often asks you to watch your breaths come and go for

half an hour and that's it—then you're on your own. But this is very hard for most of us to do. Our thoughts seem to automatically spring back into rapid-shifting work mode, and we lose the vital awareness of our breathing and whole-body presence.

This is where the traditional mantra or short, repeated saying lends a helpful hand. New cognitive insights into the process have enabled us to develop statements and other refocusing techniques that greatly enhance the recharge process, including the following:

Breath Counting: This is a very good starting point for creating mental stillness and refreshing your brain. As you stay fully aware of all the breath sensations and movements, count each exhale, one after the other, and naturally quiet your mind on the inhale. This counting combined with the focus on your breathing will almost immediately quiet the flow of thoughts through the mind, which is the shortest route to rejuvenation.

Your Own Focus Statement: Some classic phrases have been shown to be effective within this process of mental shifting. However, you're free to come up with your own variations to make the experience more personalized and meaningful to you. Often the process of inventing your own focus statement enables you to discover a special mantra that is ideally suited for you, so feel free to experiment.

You'll want to use a focus statement that aims your attention on the here and now, focusing on *sensations* rather than thoughts or memories, and encouraging relaxation rather than stress. Examples include:

"Renew, relax"   "Recharge"

"Be here, now"   "One"

"I feel light and energized"   "Calm"

"I am investing in myself"   "Clear and present"

Visual Aids for Focusing: Many people benefit from keeping their eyes open rather than closed, and looking at a beautiful picture of nature or piece of artwork that focuses their attention calmly. Just be sure you don't look at a picture that is filled with too many emotional associations, such as photos of family vacations or special events. This can lead you off into memories and imaginations that take you away from the rejuvenation of the present moment.

Audio Aids for Focusing: Quiet, non-emotional music can help in the relaxation and centering process, as long as it stays in the background and doesn't carry you away from your focus on your breathing. Likewise, guided audio sessions can be valuable if they're not too complex.

As you begin to train your brain to focus in the moment, an audio aid can help to quiet the natural tendency to shift to future and past experiences. With practice, you may find any noise to be somewhat distracting, and prefer to quiet your mind without any external guidance. Stay tuned in to your process each time you recharge, and you'll begin to discover your own best practices.

5. **Non-judgmental Attitude.** A key to success with this type of mental exercise is to keep from evaluating or judging how you're doing with the process. There is no right or

wrong here, no good or bad performance. In fact, this is not about performance at all. It's simply about shifting from one mental mode (thinking) to another (experiencing) quickly and completely.

Don't be surprised if you initially find it frustrating and difficult to quiet your mind. I remember almost yelling at myself for not being able to stop my thoughts when I first began this process. It may be helpful to have a pen and paper nearby to quickly jot down thoughts you seem to be hanging onto in order to let them go. The more you practice, the more you will realize that those thoughts will still be there when you need them in the future and that you can just acknowledge their presence and let them go. After months of practice, I have finally gotten to the point where I can say to myself, "nice thought, I'll get to you later," and let go.

In the same way that you can't make an effort to relax a physical muscle, you can't make an effort to relax your mind. You must simply choose to let go and focus attention onto an effortless, natural bodily function such as your breathing. Then you are free to enjoy the temporary peace and quiet when all thoughts stop. The more you bring attention to your breathing, quiet your mind, and recharge your mental energy, the easier it will be to create an operating system that supports optimal energy and sustainable behavior change.

Advanced Practice

As you become more familiar with this relaxation process, you may want to take it a step further by adding visualization. Studies have shown that *visualizing* an activity may be just as effective as actually *performing* that activity when it comes to training the brain. (And in case you're wondering, no, thinking about going to the gym is not the same as actually going to the gym. If only that were the case!)

For example, neuroscience pioneer Alvaro Pascual-Leone conducted a study where he gave two groups of people who had never studied piano a series of notes to play, and told them which fingers to move to hit specific keys. One group sat in front of a keyboard for two hours a day for five days, imagining playing the piano and hearing the corresponding tones. The other group actually practiced playing the piano for the same amount of time.

Brain scans were done before, during, and after the experiment, and a computer was used to measure the accuracy of the performances. By the end of the study, brain change and accuracy were the same in both groups.[5]

For the sake of our program, there are a few ways you can use this advanced type of mental training, utilizing visualization along with the relaxation response, to help you move closer to your goals. One option would be to visualize yourself making better choices about your personal energy management. Imagine yourself out to dinner with friends, ordering foods that will make you feel good, eating them in appropriate serving sizes, and thoroughly enjoying both the taste of the food and the social connection with others.

You could even use this type of visualization before returning home after work. Visualize yourself being able to turn off thoughts of the day and fully engage with your family or friends in order to shift gears to strengthen your community. Imagine specifically how it will look and feel for you to be fully focused on the people you care about, while you let go of your concerns or worries about tomorrow.

It might seem a bit intimidating at first to use these advanced practices on your own, but there are a lot of tools available to help coach you through the process. Visit my website synergyprograms.com for free audio tracks to help guide you through visualization. As you become more comfortable, you will soon find yourself finding more creative ways to train your brain to help you get where you want to go.

Recharge Tools and Strategies

It's often difficult to get a busy brain to take a break from stressful fixations. The basic process in this book will help greatly, and you might also benefit from using media tools such as audio tracks or meditation videos designed to help you effortlessly refocus your attention and minimize distracting thoughts.

I encourage you to visit the SHARP Brain Gym at synergyprograms.com/braingym to explore the excellent multimedia meditation tools that are available. My colleagues and I have developed a number of guided experiences that will help you considerably when both developing new recharge habits and moving through them regularly.

As you come to realize that you *do* indeed have a certain amount of control and freedom to maintain a calmer state of mind at work and at home, you may want to consider additional ways to provide environmental support for yourself: soft or inspirational music, beautiful photographs of calming places or friends and family, light dimmers, a desktop waterfall, or aromatherapy. You may even find that simply lighting a candle or heating up some scented oil in a burner can instantly help bring you into a more calm state of mind while at home.

stress

Training Tips:

- The body has a natural response to balance stress.
- Breathing triggers the relaxation response.
- Relaxation practice must be scheduled.
- Simple meditation can initiate the relaxation response.
- Visualization can boost relaxation benefits.

Training Techniques:

- Schedule two- to three-minute recharge breaks throughout the day.
- Do full-body stretching.
- Take a walk in nature.
- Meditate (passive or active).
- Explore relaxing visualization or guided imagery.
- Practice deep-breathing exercises.
- Laugh, play, have fun.
- Take a yoga class.
- Get a massage or other spa service.
- Practice other stress management rituals that help bring brain chemistry back into balance by initiating the relaxation response.

Training Exercise #2: Recharge

To further our habit-building theme, let's end this chapter by continuing with the mental focusing exercise already introduced—that of pausing and refocusing your attention to your breathing habits. We will expand that cognitive-shifting experience a step so that you quickly let go of multitasking and other mental stressors, and start reinforcing new habits that bring more oxygen to your brain and balance out your brain chemistry.

As we did before, begin this exercise while you continue reading by 'doing' nothing at all except refocusing your mind's attention gently toward the sensation that's happening all the time inside your body. Just tune into sensory mode in this moment, where your breath reflex is continuing to bring oxygen into your lungs and ultimately to your brain, and then blowing the used-up air out through your nose (or mouth).

Notice at first that your breathing is still operating mostly on automatic pilot. You've probably been mostly unconscious of your breathing for at least the past hour, despite the fact that how you breathe is crucial to your overall vitality and performance.

Simply be the observer as you focus your attention on your body's breathing patterns; notice how your breathing quite quickly begins to become deeper and more relaxed when you pay attention to it. This is where we find a key to habit change: When you focus your attention on a habit, you can directly perceive its effect on your body and well-being—and that very act of perceiving the effect will stimulate needed change.

For instance, as you continue to experience the sensations that are taking place right now because of your breathing—both in your nose and also in your chest and belly—notice if and when tensions begin to relax. Then recognize that as tensions relax, you feel better. This direct perception is a powerful teacher, one that's able to guide your focus in rewarding directions.

If you find your attention wandering away from your breathing and back to thinking about this and that, the following addition to the exercise will bring your attention back into the present moment, 100 percent, free of all multitasking temptations.

As you continue watching your breaths come and go, with every inhale and exhale, repeat the following words:

(exhale . . .) Relax . . . (inhale . . .) Renew

Making no effort to breathe in any particular way, repeat the words "relax, renew" as it feels comfortable, for a few minutes. Simply notice whatever cognitive shift you experience within caused by just one minute of focusing entirely on words and sensations that aim your attention on mind-body presence in the here and now. Breathe, and experience the present moment as you restore balance and recharge your energy.

3

Engage Your Heart

If you've ever had the chance to work for a highly energized CEO or other manager, you know how powerful an experience it can be. Working with a leader who is able to bring together the organization's ultimate mission while simultaneously tapping into individuals' personal missions is truly a gift. Leadership is one of the strongest factors in determining success. I've seen it drive shared missions—and crash those without a solid foundation.

Consider your heart to be the CEO of your body's operating system. Phase Two of the SHARP Solution focuses on this powerful energy generator, which will help the rest of your life— brain, mind, body, and community—work together. Like the tough task CEOs face when they align the organization's mission with those of the people working for it, aligning all of these unique components takes work, time, energy, oftentimes money, and almost always patience. Yet I would argue that it's an investment worth making. Personal engagement happens when the passions of your heart are in alignment with the focus of your mind, and the focus of your mind is in alignment with the passions of your heart. This is equivalent to getting the CEO and CFO of your operating system working on a shared mission.

In the same way, you'd have a hard time achieving your goals if you simply engaged the analytical CFO brain without a clear purpose. It is often the passionate CEO who keeps us coming back to what's ultimately most important to us. While it may not appear to call the shots on a daily basis, the heart supports the motivation that keeps us moving, and without that we would wander aimlessly. It always saddens me to find out that my clients have been spending their energy haphazardly because they weren't able to clearly define their purpose or driving force in life. As the saying goes, if you don't know where you're going, any road will get you there.

According to *The Blue Zones* author Dan Buettner, people who know why they wake up in the morning live up to seven years longer than those who don't.[1] In Okinawa, this concept is known as *ikigai*, which has been translated as "believing that one's life is worth living," "something important one lives for," or "a reason for being." We often talk about the power of purpose, but can easily find ourselves slipping back into survival mode when we feel time-crunched or overly stressed. Simple exercises help us tap into our passions, purpose, and motivation, which can fuel our efforts and give us a clearer sense of direction when it comes to investing our time and energy.

SHARP Science: Live Longer on Purpose

A recent study from Rush University Medical Center showed that people who reported greater purpose in life exhibited better cognitive functioning than those with less purpose in life, even as plaques and tangles accumulated in their brains! Though these plaques and tangles have long been associated with Alzheimer's disease, recent data suggests that they can accumulate throughout the aging process—even in individuals without brain disease—causing a disruption of memory and other mental capacities. However, having a clear sense of purpose throughout the lifespan may protect against the harmful effects of aging on the brain.[2]

Creating a Clear Vision

It is absolutely critical in reaching any goal that we first have a clear picture of what that goal is and why it's important to us. Too often, people start out focused on the *how*, for instance, the specifics around how to eat and exercise, without identifying the *why*. *What* do you want to gain from this experience? And *why* does that matter to you?

Let's start with the destination in mind. What do you want to see happen as a result of this process? If you are going to dedicate valuable time and energy to taking better care of yourself, it's going to require a significant investment. And if you're not sure where it is that you want to be when you get to the end, there is no way you're going to know how to get there. After all, we each have a unique pathway to health and well-being, and much of it is determined by where we're starting from and what matters most to us.

If you feel like you have a long journey ahead, relax. Rather than looking at the mountain that might be staring you in the face, let's just look at the journey's first few steps. What would you like to see as a result of following this program for the first two weeks? How about 30 days?

It's important to keep in mind that there are things you can control and things you can't as you think through your goals. For instance, while you can control your behavior, you can't control the outcome, or result of that behavior. Let me explain.

Anyone who has ever tried to lose weight knows that it can be a very frustrating process. You can choose to eat less, move more, relax regularly, sleep well, be social—in other words, you can do *everything* you're supposed to do—and the scale may stay right where it is, or (gasp) even go up. That's reality. But if your goal is focused on the behavior and not the outcome, you still win.

If you're able to stay focused and relaxed even during plateaus, you will be aware of the other benefits of your efforts: increased energy, alertness, focus, creativity, and happiness. Eventually, the results in your physical body shaping will come through your consistent practice. And most importantly, these results will be significant, not superficial or temporary.

You don't have to set a specific behavioral goal yet; we will do that once we walk through each of the techniques. However, we can take a look at the final destination by creating a vision statement. Visualize how you want to feel at the end of this first 30 days. Do you want to be lighter? More energized? More focused? Do you want to have more clarity? Be more creative? Inspired?

Take a few moments to create your own vision statement. If you find yourself getting stuck, do not worry—that's exactly what we don't want to happen. Reach out to us at coach@synergyprograms.com and we can provide additional tools to help you or even set you up with one of our trained coaches to provide some assistance.

Give it a try now: At the end of this 30-day process, I will

_____ .

Your Purpose Statement

Now that you have a clear vision for what you want to see happen as a result of your efforts, you must be very clear about your motivation for making such a big investment in yourself. It is going to take time and energy. You will need to set new priorities for yourself, and make some adjustments that are probably going to be temporarily uncomfortable. There will be techniques that challenge you, and of course obstacles that pop up along the way and make it difficult to keep moving forward. These are the moments when you absolutely must know—and remind yourself—*why* you're on this journey in the first place, so that you can quickly get right back on track.

Your sense of purpose ultimately provides the driving force for your behavior; this is true for anything you do in life. If you say you want to do something but it's not truly aligned with what's most important to you, you will never be successful in the long run. Let me give you an example of what I'm talking about here.

A husband decides to go on a diet, because he's tired of hearing about his weight from his nagging spouse. Even though he doesn't consider those few extra pounds to be a big deal (not to mention that his wife isn't exactly in tip-top shape either), he agrees to eat more healthfully and hit the gym more often. When mealtime comes around and he realizes that he *should* order a half portion, a little voice inside says, "You deserve to eat all of this. You've had a long day. You're tired. It's not that big a deal if you do it just this once."

Although this man has the best intentions, he quickly becomes absorbed in just getting things done, and cleans his plate before he knows it. This is where the voice really kicks in, "You can just start tomorrow." or "You knew you couldn't do it, so why bother?" Those voices are always present and may continue to be, but without a clear sense of purpose, there is nothing to fight them off. There is no replacement script or message to argue back.

Consider another example: This same husband decides that he's tired of feeling like he has no energy, and that it's time for him to take some time for himself, to nurture his own energy so that he has more to give to the people about whom he cares the most. He's clear that his purpose in participating in a wellness program isn't really about losing the weight, although it's not a bad side effect. His primary goal is to feel better physically, to have more energy, to be more clear-headed and able to be fully engaged with his family at the end of the day. He is able to connect how he feels by getting in touch with the quality of love he expresses to his children. He wants to be the very best father possible during the precious time he has while his kids are still at home. The voice is still there; but this time it's not alone.

"You deserve to eat this. You've had a long day. You're tired. It's not that big a deal, just this once," the voice says.

But this time, the husband has another voice fighting back. "It's not about deserving food; I deserve to *feel good*. The right food will energize me so that I can do other things that I truly enjoy—things that nurture me more than this food ever could. Each choice is a big deal, because each choice gives me the chance to make a better choice than I did last time, helping to create a new habit."

Before we get too far ahead of ourselves with voices and stories, let's take a moment to determine *your* true purpose for going on this wellness journey. What are your core values, and how do they play a role in your underlying reason for wanting to create new supportive behaviors? No matter what the desired outcome, a clear objective will help you generate the motivation and staying power to keep you moving you forward on your journey, in the direction of your most important goals.

Some common core values that are connected to wellness include:

Family

Health

Community

Environment

Financial security

Emotional stability

Happiness

Relationship

Self-esteem

Career

Faith

Are any other values (not listed above) an important part of this process for you?

Once you've identified the contributing factors to your purpose, you can begin to create a purpose statement or personal mantra. This will be essential to keeping you motivated and creating the right story for success. A purpose statement simply requires that you put your reason for going on this journey into words. For instance:

- I want to be healthier so that I can feel more energized at the end of the day and able to play with my kids more regularly.
- I want to practice recovery more often so that I can be an example to my clients of how taking care of oneself first is necessary in caring for others.

- I want to lose weight so I can take less medicine, secure a healthier future, and save money for myself and my family.
- I want to be happier so I can experience more joy in my relationship, and be more positive around my family.
- I want to take better care of myself because my faith tells me that the body is a temple, and I want to take better care of that temple.
- Now it's your turn. Keep in mind that this is not a one-time statement; your purpose may change in 30 days, or it may change tomorrow. You can rewrite it at any time. The important thing is that you stay clear about what it is, feel motivated by it, and are able to connect to it on a regular basis.
- I want to _____ because _____

What's Your Story?

Let's get back to those voices we were talking about earlier. They're the ones that are asking you right at this moment, "What the heck is she talking about?" Whether we're aware of it or not, we all have a constant internal dialogue taking place in our minds. The conversations consist of the things we say to ourselves and about ourselves; sometimes they're intentional, but many times they're not. Quite often, we aren't even aware of the messages that we're sending and receiving—let alone the significant impact they're having.

Here's an example: You're sitting at the table eating dinner when you realize you've had enough to eat. There is still food on the plate, and you know you *could* eat more; but you also recognize that you *should* just stop and save the extra calories. You think about pushing the plate away when you suddenly picture your mother or father telling you once again about the starving children in other countries. They remind you of how grateful you should be that you have this food, and encourage you to clean your plate. You don't want to be wasteful, and you certainly don't want to offend anyone—whether it's your host, a waiter or waitress, or the person who cooked (which might be you, in which case you worked hard to make the meal in the first place and don't want to waste it). So, you do what most of us would do. You decide to clean your plate—after all, you enjoy eating the food—and you just unbutton your pants at the end of the meal in satisfaction, possibly with a side of guilt.

That's the voice I'm talking about. It might be your voice, or someone else's—a parent's, a Sunday school teacher's, a friend's, or a combination of all of them. It really doesn't matter who's talking. What *does* matter is that you recognize that this same voice directs your actions, whether you're aware of it or not. But it doesn't have to.

You have the choice to change the messaging, to create a new script, and ultimately write a new story for yourself. You have to be aware of what the message is, rewrite it, and practice it over and over again until it becomes the new voice. This is simply a way of retraining your brain to work differently; something that's entirely possible if you have the motivation and are willing to do the work.

SHARP Science: Stories Shape Perception

A recent study demonstrated that how you perceive others may say a lot about the kind of person you are. Researchers at the University of Nebraska-Lincoln found

(*continued*)

that participants who imagined positive co-workers contributed more in the workplace, both in job performance and in terms of going above and beyond their job descriptions to help others. According to lead researcher Peter Harms, the study targeted "psychological capital"—a cluster of personality characteristics associated with the ability to overcome potential obstacles and actively pursue one's goals. By using projective storytelling, researchers were able to predict real-life work outcomes based on an individual's perceptions of the world around them. "When you make up imaginary peers, they are completely a product of how you see the world," Harms said. This allows us to gain better insight into perceptual biases.[3]

Let's look at that very common story of cleaning your plate. I am like most people I know in that I hate throwing food away. Food is good. I like how it tastes and how it makes me feel, and it bothers me to think about wasting it. I am also well aware of how blessed I am to have food, and I don't like to think that other people perceive that I'm taking it for granted.

This is all very true. However, there is another element of truth that always seems to be missing from this simple story. The fact is, too much food is wasteful whether we eat it or not. If I eat more than I need, I'm still wasting it; the difference is that I carry around the evidence of my wastefulness for everyone to see and for me to feel. If it's more than I need, I really should be sharing it with someone who needs it. And I'm occasionally able to do this, whether by sharing a meal or giving away my leftovers.

However, even when that is not an option there really are only two ways this story can end: I throw the food away and accept that it's more than I needed (or save it for later, which is always my preference when I'm not traveling), or I eat the extra food, which is still more than I need, but I tell myself I'm not wasting it and I end up storing it on my waist. Put simply, we either *waste* it or we *waist* it. The choice is ours.

Once I realized this, I was able to engage in a very different internal dialogue and enjoy a very different outcome. It was a huge turning point in my own wellness journey. I realized that throwing food away is often a necessity if you want to be healthy. And after years of struggling with my weight, it was just one of many stories that I've had to rewrite for myself to be able to create healthy, sustainable habits.

So, what's *your* story? What messages are you telling yourself that might be hindering your own success? You may not be able to identify all of them right from the start. However, once you become more aware of the stories you tell yourself about yourself, you'll be better able to create and practice a new script, and write a new story.

Think of one behavior you've tried to change in the past. Engage in the process of identifying the story, rewriting it, and then practicing it to see if you can make it stick. Remember to connect it to your purpose statement so that you remain emotionally motivated to keep working at it.

Let's practice: What behavior have you tried to add or change in the past that you were not able to do successfully? (Eat breakfast, sleep more, exercise regularly, take breaks, connect with co-workers, send a handwritten note to clients, etc.)

Say to yourself, "I want to _____" (fill in the blank with the behavior change). What reason do you give for why you couldn't or can't? What is the big BUT that impedes your success?

I want to _____,

but _____.

You may start to recognize this as an excuse, and it might be, but there is likely some truth to it as well. The key to rewriting an old story is to determine if it's moving you in the direction you want to go, and if it's completely true. Are you leaving any facts out?

Again, don't worry if this is challenging for you. Reach out to us for more tools on rewriting your story or, to discuss this process with a personal coach, email coach@synergyprograms.com.

Once you have created a personal vision statement for yourself, identified your purpose statement, and started to rewrite your story, you're ready for the next step in our journey: focusing your mind. Remember, you don't want to stress yourself out over any of these steps, since that will slow down the process. Relax and enjoy each step of the journey.

Before we move on to our next technique, let's take a break to boost the feel good chemicals in your brain as we continue to prepare to build a healthier, happier mind and body.

Training Tips:
- Purpose, passion, and motivation are matters of the heart.
- Start with the destination in mind.
- Purpose drives behavior.
- A purpose statement may evolve over time.
- Our story moves us forward or holds us back.

Training Techniques:

- Write your purpose statement each morning before you start your day.
- Read your purpose statement out loud at key times throughout the day.
- Place motivational statements or photographs in your environment and reflect on them regularly.
- Subscribe to a blog, newsletter, or email that reminds you to think about your purpose (such as our SHARP Strategies group on LinkedIn).
- Plan to call home at a certain time each day to connect with family.
- Engage in spiritual practices such as prayer or reading scripture.
- Read inspirational books or stories to start or finish the day.
- Discuss the importance of purpose with family or friends.
- Keep a daily journal recording times you felt "on purpose" or "in the zone" throughout the day.
- Create an inspirational ringtone that will remind you of your purpose each time you receive a phone call.

Training Exercise #3: Laugh

Laughter's benefits have been well documented over time; in the 18th century, French writer Sebastian Chamfort wrote, "The most wasted day is one in which we have not laughed." Famous editor and writer Norman Cousins

(continued)

Training Exercise #3: Laugh (*Continued*)

explained in his best seller, *Anatomy of an Illness*, how laughter helped him overcome the pain of his severely debilitating disease of the endocrine system. "I made the joyous discovery that ten minutes of genuine belly laughter had an anesthetic effect and would give me at least two hours of pain-free sleep." Part of the therapy he designed for himself included watching Marx Brothers movies and reading humor books.[4]

There are many ways to add laughter to your routine, including watching funny videos online or joining a laughter group. After all, laughter is contagious; when you see someone else laughing, mirror neurons in your brain light up and give you the sensation of finding something funny so that you too may start to giggle. Try it now by visiting our Laugh Out Loud page, www.synergyprograms.com/LOL.

© Randy Glasbergen.
www.glasbergen.com

"Many people believe that laughter is the best medicine, so the government has declared a ban on all laughing until further studies can be done."

Sometimes the best thing you can do for both your body and your brain is simply to *laugh*. There's a reason that laughter is considered the best medicine, and laughter therapy, groups, and clubs have sprouted up all over the country to help people improve their health and happiness. It's a bit disheartening to think that we have to designate specific laughing time; but just like everything else we're talking about in this book, if you don't plan it, it's not going to happen. Yes, we may laugh during the day from time to time, but because we are so busy, most of us hardly slow down long enough to allow ourselves to have a good, satisfying belly laugh.

Laughter is beneficial in multiple ways. Physically, it stimulates most of the same endorphins (brain chemicals) as exercise and can increase blood flow and energy production. Mentally, it helps us get a nice break from stress and stimulates the relaxation response inside our body and mind. Laughter even boosts our social connection by stimulating the hormone oxytocin, which helps us feel more bonded to those around us.

SHARP Science: Monkey Love

We have long known that the brain chemical oxytocin creates social bonds between individuals. It turns out that this love hormone may also be a beneficial treatment for brain disorders that lead to a disinterest in others, such

(*continued*)

as some forms of autism or schizophrenia. Researchers at Duke University administered the oxytocin hormone nasally through a small nebulizer (like a gas mask) to macaque monkeys. The inhaled oxytocin enhanced pro-social choices by the monkeys, such as providing a reward to other monkeys even when they didn't receive one themselves. Not only were researchers able to see a clear increase in kindness between monkeys; they were also able to determine that nasally administered oxytocin actually travels into the brain. This method of delivery may be better for treating children with autism or other related disorders more comfortably and effectively than previous nasal sprays.[5]

Focus Your Mind

Phase Three of the SHARP Solution focuses on the mind. It has been said that we only spend about 10 percent of our time in the current moment, 50 percent anticipating what's ahead of us, and 40 percent reflecting on what's behind us. This makes sense from a caveman perspective, as our survival-based focus prepares for the future and learns from the past. But when it really counts, we need to be entirely present in the current moment. In order to give energy to the people and things that matter most to us, we need to be very clear about where we choose to focus our attention.

Considering the fact that we have approximately 60,000 thoughts every single day, and that each thought that catches our attention requires us to spend energy, it's no wonder that we feel as if we're running on fumes by the end of the day. The more we have on our mind at any given moment, the more energy we use to operate our brainpower. Fortunately, we can control where we choose to direct our attention and how much time and effort we spend on each thought.

So, how can you better manage your mental energy so you can meet your daily demands? The following are three ways you can keep your energy tank full and readily available when you need it.

1. **Spend wisely.** The first step in managing your mental energy is to be more aware of how you're using it. Most people are so busy during the day they fail to even consider

that they might be spending beyond their limit, which often leads to burnout and fatigue. Try to avoid spending carelessly by bringing more mindful attention to each present moment; this can help keep you from drifting along aimlessly. You can practice mindfulness in specific, scheduled sessions, or you can bring it to certain events throughout the day such as during mealtimes, on a commute, while waiting for an appointment or preparing for a meeting. No matter where or when you decide to do it, the more you practice being mindful, the easier it will be to focus your attention on only the things that matter most to you in each moment.

2. **Conserve when necessary.** Sometimes you can't avoid giving attention to multiple priorities at the same time. It's the nature of our busy, constantly connected, on-the-go society. However, we know that multitasking dumbs us down and wears us out quickly, because we're giving the brain more demands than it can meet in that moment. When you're dealing with too much at once, try chunking your day into shorter sections of time that let you shift from multitasking to multi-*prioritizing*. This allows you to give each priority its own, specific, focused time slot. Even if they're only five-minute blocks, scheduling your day in chunks sets specific boundaries, which allows you to better utilize your brain, instead of constantly shifting back and forth. When thoughts that require attention pop up, quickly jot them down and go back to them when your focus time is over so you can schedule specific time to pay attention to the new task.

3. **Invest strategically.** It's important to recognize that the same energy source fuels our brainpower and our body. This means that you will deplete the energy that's available for your mental demands if you don't invest in your physical energy throughout the day. As we will discuss at length in Chapter 5, you must eat high-quality food every three to four hours to keep glucose levels steady, a requirement for both physical and mental performance. Taking breaks to get short bursts of physical activity each hour keeps circulation going strong so that oxygen can be delivered to the body and the brain. Even just 30 seconds of standing, walking, or doing squats gets your blood pumping enough to provide a quick energy boost. Ideally, you should aim for about five minutes each hour to turn off your mind and engage your body for optimal brainpower.

Always remember that attention is something you have to pay for with your energy. You can maximize your energy account if you're mindful of how you're spending, conserve when necessary, and invest in your energy supply throughout the day. This way, you'll have what you need—not only to meet your daily demands, but also to give energy to the people and activities that matter most to you.

Multitasking and Our Monkey Brain

With so many demands on your mental energy, it's easy to find yourself being pulled in multiple directions. Jumping from one project to another may seem like the only option for getting things done; however, the negative impact on attention and focus is significant and stressful to the brain. Although we claim that being "good at multitasking" is part of our job description, we need to change the way we tackle multiple priorities so that we can focus our mental energy on those things that *really* require our attention.

While this approach may appear to take longer, the fact is that we can actually get more done in the time we have. This ends up saving us precious time in the long run, increases our productivity and performance, and keeps our brain in a more relaxed and focused state.

The truth is that our brain is wired in a way that only *allows* it to focus on one thing at a time. Consider the simple example of juggling. It may appear that you're doing several tasks at once, but you can only focus on one ball at a time—the rest are just floating in the air. The time it takes to switch our attention back and forth between tasks substantially reduces our efficiency. In addition to slowing us down, it puts unnecessary stress on our system, leading us to make more errors in our performance while our bodies produce higher levels of unhealthy cortisol.

In a recent study, participants who completed two simultaneous tasks took up to 30 percent longer and made twice as many errors as those who completed the same tasks in sequence.[1] When we switch tasks, we have to turn our attention away from one task and then determine or recall the rules for completing the next task. Time-management experts believe that it can take approximately 20 minutes to fully recover from shifting attention, and the time increases for more complex tasks. Think about how challenging it can be to get back into the creative flow after you've been distracted by a co-worker, a phone call, or watching your email inbox accumulate messages.

Anyone who's ever become distracted while reading understands what happens when you lose your attention for even a moment: Your mind wanders and you have to flip back a few pages to figure out where you left off.

Another problem with multitasking is that it forces us to respond quickly, without time to assess the situation, consider multiple options, and then mindfully make a decision. As we discussed earlier, this situation forces us to use our monkey brain. Multitaskers also show higher levels of stress hormones than their more single-minded counterparts. Researchers at Reuters found that two-thirds of respondents believed that information overload had decreased job satisfaction and damaged their personal relationships, while one-third believed it had damaged their health.[2] The added stress of multitasking can increase the production of stress hormones, which damage brain cells over time.

People who multitask too much often experience various warning signs: foggy short-term memory, difficulty concentrating, or gaps in attentiveness. And the office isn't the only place where multitasking can hurt us. Staying focused on one task at a time also benefits our personal relationships, as we are more able to pay full attention to the people with whom we're spending time.

Of course, it may be unavoidable to encounter certain situations that require multitasking. I have worked with many executive assistants who are required to stop in the middle of a task the moment their boss needs attention. An employee at a call center or a busy medical office may need to quickly shift from one assignment to the next. A parent with more than one child certainly knows how important it is to be able to split focus to be in full protection mode. We're often able to tone our multitasking muscles through practice, stress management, and a good self-care regimen that provides us with proper nutrition, physical activity, and adequate sleep. This makes the need to handle multiple priorities a bit easier, and keeps from breaking us down as much as it might if our systems were weaker. It's not *ideal*, of course; but sometimes it's the only option.

"It doesn't mean you can't do several things at the same time," says Dr. Marcel Just, co-director of Carnegie Mellon University's Center for Cognitive Brain Imaging. "But we're kidding ourselves if we think we can do so without cost." Your attention comes at a cost: your energy. The concept of *paying* attention is right on, and it's critical to consider how you're investing in your ability to guide your attention in the directions that are most important to you. And it can be just as important to learn what *not* to pay attention to when it comes to your energy management strategies.

SHARP Science: Anticipation Costs Attention

We all know that using cell phones while driving is dangerous. However, a recent study shows that even *anticipating* calls or messages may distract drivers, thereby increasing the risk of a crash. Researchers at the University of Washington enlisted 384 students to complete the Cell Phone Overuse Scale (CPOS), a 24-item assessment that determines four aspects of problematic cell phone use:

1. Frequent anticipation of calls/messages
2. Interference with normal activities

3. A strong emotional reaction to the cell phone
4. Recognizing problem use

Of these four dimensions, a higher level of call anticipation was significantly associated with prior crashes. To
stay safe, use the same rule that's applied to air travel; turn
the phone *off* (not on silent or vibrate).[3]

There are hundreds of external stimuli that compete for
our attention at any given time. Focusing your mental energy in
ways that best move you along your mission requires that you
also learn how to ignore the things that might pull you off
course. Just like strength training at the gym, learning to resist a
pull on your attention can strengthen your ability to keep your
mind in the present moment. There are a few simple ways to
strengthen your distraction resistance muscle throughout the
day: Turn it off, tune it out, or take a time out.

First, if at all possible, create an environment that supports
your ability to focus your full attention on the present moment.
Turn off background noise, turn away from distracting activity,
and eliminate the pull of the electronic leashes we call computers and smartphones. While these helpful tools often act as a
spare brain, they can also zap our energy and immediately take
us away from the moment, leading us to use our monkey brain
once again.

You can practice tuning out the noise by setting a timer
for a short period, maybe three to five minutes to begin, and
focusing completely on one task. The more you practice full
engagement in the moment, the more mentally tough you

will become—even in the midst of a chaotic environment. Finally, when all else fails and the distractions feel overwhelming, take a time out and just walk away for a bit. Getting some physical activity, talking to a co-worker or friend for a few minutes to shift out of work mode, or doing a short brain recharge can help you regain your focus and invest mental energy to get back on track.

Time management is another important strategy when it comes to getting things done. However, it's not just the time that we need to manage. The mental energy we give to the time that we have determines how productive that time will be. Each activity upon which we chose to focus throughout the day requires attention—supported by our energy—which means our CFO brain has to allot adequate resources. Take on too many tasks or objects of focus at once and the brain will become overwhelmed, triggering a stress response, slowing us down, and ultimately wearing us out.

To avoid multitasking, chunk your day into blocks that allow you to focus more specifically and purposefully during that time frame. The length of time can vary, as long as you plan ahead of time and schedule movement breaks at least every 90 minutes to keep your focus. Breaking big projects down into smaller steps, a strategy called chunking, can also help you avoid getting distracted by the big picture or feeling overwhelmed. This goes a long way in keeping creativity flowing on a lengthier project like developing a presentation, building a strategic plan, or writing a book. Instead of plugging away hour after hour, you can divide your time strategically. Keep in mind that you may need to shorten the time blocks as the day goes on to help manage and maintain focus as your energy levels naturally decline a bit.

Mindfulness Matters

Just like the muscles in our body, we need a strategy to help us build better mental capacities like focus, concentration, and attention. Although many of us have trained ourselves to be pretty good at multitasking—and regularly fall into this pattern on automatic pilot—we can create a new way of doing things by utilizing the training strategies of cognitive fitness. In her book *Rapt*, author Winifred Gallagher reminds us, "Most failures occur despite effort, not due to a lack of it."[4] It's not about working longer hours or trying harder; it's about bringing the best energy we have to the time we have. Mental focus and attention are crucial to making sure that happens.

SHARP Science: Too Much of a Good Thing?

Despite the fact that most people consider multitasking a necessary skill for today's complex work environment, our brains simply aren't designed to deal with several tasks at once. It turns out that we may have even more reason to feel pulled to multitask. In a study at Ohio State University, college students reported feeling more emotionally satisfied when they watched TV while reading a book, even though their cognitive performance of both activities was hindered. Researchers found that as mental demands went up, students sought out multiple media outlets such as web browsing, radio, and television to meet their

(continued)

SHARP Science: Too Much of a Good Thing? (*Continued*)

emotional needs (e.g., fun, entertainment, relaxation). Although the multitasking clearly hindered their cognitive performance, the emotional support they experience strengthens neural connections, creating a dynamic feedback loop that encourages multitasking in the future.[5]

An important consideration here is the impact of constant stimuli on the brain. With so many things competing for our attention at any particular time, the brain's job is to determine what is important and what we can ignore. We are often unaware of how much media stimulation bombards us throughout the day. Phone calls and email may be obvious, but think about today's supercharged advertisements, with constant scrolling data along the bottom of our screens, pop-up ads, and noisy videos in the sidebars of webpages. Even just the noise in our environment—the hustle and bustle of daily life—can require a bit of mental energy to determine if it's worth paying attention to or not. Imagine you took the time to notice *everything* around you at one time; you'd have an attention debt for sure. Our ability to tune out the unnecessary is critical for our brain to maintain optimal functioning.

Mindfulness is a state of being that has been associated with many different behaviors and self-healing. One of the most researched techniques is Mindfulness Based Stress Reduction (MSBR), developed by John Kabat-Zinn at the University of Massachusetts Medical School. Although traditional mindfulness practice is rooted in Buddhist teachings, MBSR does not

require a spiritual component. Rather, it is a clinically standard-
ized meditation that has shown consistent efficacy for many
mental and physical disorders. MBSR and other mindfulness
practices have demonstrated the ability to reduce stress and
anxiety in many quality studies. In one seven-week mindfulness
intervention, the treatment group displayed marked reduction
in depression, anxiety, anger, and confusion over the control
group.[6]

The treatment group also had fewer overall symptoms of
stress, cardiopulmonary, and gastrointestinal symptoms, less
emotional irritability and cognitive disorganization, and fewer
habitual patterns of stress. Overall reduction in total mood
disturbance was 65 percent with a 31 percent reduction in symptoms of stress.

MBSR participation was associated with enhanced quality
of life, decreased stress symptoms, altered cortisol, and immune
patterns consistent with less stress and mood disturbance and
decreased blood pressure. MBSR has been shown to positively
impact the immune system's functioning, decrease anxiety and
depression, and increase happiness, flow, and enjoyment of life.
Many medical facilities have also used MBSR as a less invasive
way of healing patients with chronic pain.

Mindfulness meditation and mindful eating are two other
forms of self-care. These practices focus on nourishing the
body and mind with a sense of awareness in and full enjoyment of the present moment's experience. Mindfulness practices are often described as focusing on the ability to shift
from *doing* to *being*.

Biofeedback is an excellent tool to assist with mindfulness
practice, as it provides immediate feedback on your ability to
navigate your thoughts and emotions. It can also help busy

professionals become centered by giving them something specific to focus on. Additionally, it can be fun—almost like a game—to watch the monitor change, especially for those who are more analytical in nature.

SHARP Science: Healthy Brainwashing?

New uses of EEG neurofeedback may cultivate brain states that make us highly susceptible to new messages—a situation that allows enhanced learning to take place. We have long heard of subliminal messages being used to promote positive change, such as smoking cessation or weight loss. Now, new studies have shown how to specifically apply this type of learning. A recent article in the journal *Biofeedback* presented the science and research that developed this "twilight learning" technology in the 1970's. According to several studies, an EEG range of 4–7 Hertz has been found to indicate the *theta*, the hyper-suggestible state somewhere in between wakefulness and sleep. As neurofeedback continues to develop, new projects will continue to provide evidence of what subliminal stimulation can do, exploring areas such as physical healing.[7]

Turning Mindfulness into Mindsight

Mental focusing exercises such as meditation not only help you increase awareness, but also harness your attention in directions that will best serve you. This works best if you undergo a two-step process: First, create awareness through mindfulness; and then, tune into your mindsight. The term *mindsight* was created by neuroscientist Dan Siegel to describe our ability to use mental energy to direct the activities of the mind. As stated on Dr. Siegel's website (www.drdansiegel.com/about/mindsight/), "Mindsight is a kind of focused attention that allows us to see the internal workings of our own minds." Simply put, using your mind to consciously direct your attention. This unique ability to conduct our own energy is something that requires focused practice, which means spending some of our time and energy resources. However, it's one of the most important skills you can incorporate into your health, happiness, and performance routine. By using mindsight, we can become aware of how our mind is currently operating, determine if it's moving us in the direction of our goals, and, if not, change the direction to a new focus. Let me give you an example.

In simple meditation we begin by closing the eyes, relaxing the body, and tuning into our breath to initiate the relaxation response (as we did in Chapter 1's Training Exercise #1). We then work to quiet the mind and become aware of our present-moment sensations (Chapter 2's Training Exercise #2). With practice, we learn to quiet the mind and let go of the random thoughts that may arise; we simply allow them to pass through, without judging or attempting to hold onto them. We keep our focus *here* during mindfulness meditation, simply being in the moment and trying to calm the body and quiet the mind. This exercise can be both healing and energizing, as it helps us to restore balance in our brain chemistry while recovering priceless energy.

Mindsight meditation takes the exercise one step further by having us focus our attention in a particular direction; one that brings us a desired outcome such as positivity, gratitude, joy, patience, or relaxation regarding a particular challenge or concern. I do this while I fly on a plane to help calm my nerves, as I'm what they call a white-knuckle flier. I not only use short meditation to bring my body and mind to a place of calmness; I also focus my energy on visualizing the bumps of turbulence as potholes or speed bumps on a street. The twists and turns no longer represent the frightening truth that I'm up in the air in a big hunk of metal (which is where my mind initially goes), but create an image that I'm driving in a jeep through back roads in Hawaii traveling to a gorgeous remote spa. Yes, I might be a tad disappointed when I end up in a conference center instead of a resort, but the visualization leads my mind to a better place in the moment so that I can cope with the anxiety that once kept me from being able to fly.

A more common example: learning to be okay with *not* being busy. Because this is a tough one for most people I know, I have created a specific guided meditation just for this purpose. After bringing the body and mind to a relaxed, balanced state, you begin to focus your mental energy on visualizing your own internal energy tank filling up with each inhale and flowing through your body with each exhale, providing you with an abundance of energy to give to others. Rather than crashing on the couch at the end of the day, you see yourself at home—having a glass of wine, talking with your spouse, or playing with your children—feeling fully energized and completely engaged. Or, at a networking event, you can imagine that, instead of dragging yourself through the event, the experience will actually invigorate you and lead to new opportunities—all because you had the energy you needed to be present.

Using mindsight meditation has several beneficial effects. You restore healthy balance and connection between the brain and body, and consciously direct your attention to areas that activate neural connections in your brain to rewire new desired ways of thinking or being. With practice, these strengthened mental pathways will actually bring you more quickly into a state of mind that helps you reach your goals. While it initially took me several minutes to visualize the "bumpy roads" while I was up in the sky, it now occurs within a matter of seconds, as if it's my brain's preferred way of operating. Rather than immediately turning to visions of fear and disaster to try to prepare me for danger, my brain is able to shift into a more optimistic, flexible, and supportive state that helps me grow stronger through challenges rather than breaking down.

You may find it helpful to write out a script for a simple mindsight meditation that you can read or record to help direct your experience. We have several examples on our website (www.synergyprograms.com) and can provide you with a template for a meditation script to help get you started.

Makeover Your Mindset

As we become more aware of our mental energy and attention, we can begin to shift its focus into directions that better serve us on a regular basis. With practice, we're able to transform our overall perspective from a negative, survival-based one to a more positive, opportunity-based outlook. Since our primary need is to survive threats to our system, it makes sense that our mind has a tendency to focus on the negatives around us. Sure, positive things can make us temporarily happy; but it's the constant threat of danger that really keeps us on high alert.

We frequently go with our automatic response in these situations and fail to recognize that we have a choice in the story we tell ourselves. The voice we *choose* to listen to is the one that ultimately guides our behavior. Although this voice or story seems to be fixed, the reality of brain plasticity is that we can adapt our thought process by choosing a new story—and we can create a new automatic response by repeatedly practicing it.

You can train your brain to see things more positively by exercising your mindset. For example, you force your brain to focus on what's good when you write down the nice things that happen in your day. You scan the world around you looking for those things that bring you joy instead of focusing on those that bring you pain or discomfort. The more often you do this type of optimistic soul searching, the more your brain releases chemicals that make positive connections stronger—and before you know it, focusing on the positive becomes more automatic. Because our brain can only pay attention to one thing at a time, operating with a positive mindset leaves very little energy to spend on the negative, which creates a more positive lens through which we view our lives over time.

Having a more positive outlook not only contributes to happiness, but it may also help you live longer. According to a study published in the *Journal of Social Psychology*, older individuals with more positive perceptions of aging based on studies conducted up to 23 years earlier, lived 7.5 years longer than those with less positive perspectives on aging.[8]

The key message here is that we experience what we perceive, and focusing on the wrong thing can completely change what we see, *literally*. As the great psychologist William James once said, "My experience is what I agree to attend to." Training our brain to have a positive, growth-oriented, opportunity-based mindset provides flexibility training, which compels us to be resilient in complex situations and see the positive in even the most challenging of circumstances. It also decreases our knee-jerk reactions to events in our lives that spike unhealthy cortisol levels so that we can be in our optimal energy and performance zone.

By creating a more positive mindset, we prepare ourselves to interpret difficulties in life as challenges instead of threats. When we see a particular stressor, such as public speaking (oddly, for most people, a fear greater than death) or flying, as something we can *accommodate* without having to invest a great deal of energy, our physiological response is more similar to that of an acute emergency. Imagine you're on an airplane that suddenly drops (just about my least favorite thing). You have an instant surge of adrenaline, which is the primary hormonal response to an immediate need for energy; you must fight or flee. You probably feel a rush of energy, heightened senses, and enhanced short-term memory, all of which occurs to help you navigate your way out of the emergency. When you perceive a stressor as a *challenge* rather than a threat, your hormones respond in a similar way, giving you the energy you need to tackle it. As we will discuss in Chapter 5, our system experiences even exercise as a threat. Studies have suggested that forced exercise loses many of its health benefits, perhaps due to the negative impact of the stress hormones it causes the unwilling body to release. It turns out feeling like a rat on a treadmill really *isn't* that good for us after all!

In contrast, people with a fixed mindset tend to be more sensitive to the negative events they experience and more aware of needs to protect themselves for long-term survival. This is similar to people suffering from chronic stress. They believe that they're not equipped to deal with a negative situation at hand, which makes it impossible for them to resolve the problem and move past it. Take, for example, a stock market crash. The shock of what occurred may initially feel like an acute stress, but eventually, you are left in financial turmoil, which may last for a long time, keeping your system on high alert.

Feeling like you are unprepared to handle a problem, being unsure of where to turn, and sensing that you are all alone to fend for yourself in this big world is a chronic and potentially long-term situation. As a result, cortisol calls the shots in the brain, and this triggers a much different physiological response than adrenaline. Whereas adrenaline prepares you for fight or flight, cortisol prepares you to hunker down and protect yourself. Instead of needing a quick spurt of energy, cortisol works to increase glucose in the bloodstream and store it away for future needs. This is one of the reasons why stress has been linked to excess fat storage: It not only stimulates a desire for comfort and distraction, but also pushes the brain into energy-storage mode.

In what appears to be a protective mechanism, cortisol causes an inflammatory response, which is initially beneficial. It's a lot like what happens when our muscles become inflamed in response to an injury. However, cortisol's inflammatory response wears away at our system over time, injuring the tissues that make up our arteries and organs, and even destroying brain cells. Inflammation has been linked to a whole host of illnesses and diseases, including some of the biggest threats like heart disease, diabetes, cancer, Alzheimer's disease, and other forms of dementia. Perhaps the most fascinating thing about this scenario is that a simple shift in our mindset can change our physiological response, making us feel *challenged* (and releasing harmless adrenaline) rather than *threatened* (and releasing inflammatory cortisol).

This is often based on our perception of what's called our *locus of control*; that is, our belief that we can make an impact on the situation at hand, rather than feeling helpless. One particular study of 7,400 employees found that people who believed they had little control over the deadlines that other people had imposed had a 50 percent higher risk of coronary heart disease than their counterparts.[9]

Unfortunately, many of us function in survival mode throughout the day, and are not mindful of how our brains perceive what's happening around us. We're stuck in a state of self-preservation, so we tend to see the negative, potentially threatening aspects of our environment rather than stopping to relish in positive experiences. But our brain is an amazing system. It can become our greatest ally if we learn to treat it well and train it right.

Cross-Train Your Brain

As we discussed earlier, the brain is designed to spend a portion of time and energy:

- Thinking and problem solving
- Perceiving and enjoying bodily experience
- Feeling emotions and relating
- Focusing inward toward relaxation and peace

We spend the vast majority of our time on thinking and problem solving. When I think of the analogy of the brain being similar to a muscle, I can't help but picture the people I've seen at the gym who clearly spend all of their time training one part of their body. As a result, they not only appear physically out of proportion; they're also off balance and weak in certain areas, a kind of misalignment that can actually cause a host of problems. And continuing to train one particular area over and over again decreases your recovery time and increases risk of overuse injuries. This can cause the brain to experience chronic stress and fatigue, inflammation, foggy memory, and diminished performance and productivity.

If we find ourselves in survival mode while performing necessary daily tasks, we will become stuck with a thinking and problem-solving focus. We overtrain and eventually wear out that area of our cognitive functioning, while letting others atrophy. We can prevent this by performing exercises that allow us to shift out of thinking mode and into the other mental modes (i.e., enjoying bodily experience, feeling emotions, and relaxing). These cross-training exercises activate the parts of our brain that our habitual training efforts often leave behind.

Biofeedback is a specific type of exercise that can help you become more tuned into your brain-body connection. It also teaches you how to use relaxation and other mental processes to control physiological responses such as breathing and heart rate. My favorite biofeedback tool is an incredibly easy-to-use program called My Calm Beat, created by a research-based company called Brain Resource. It provides a guided process for you to discover your ideal breathing rate while practicing relaxation techniques and tracking *heart rate variability* (HRV). HRV is a measure of the continuous inter-play between the two balancing systems we discussed earlier: the sympathetic nervous system (which you can think of as your energy gas pedal) and parasympathetic nervous system (your energy brake). The human system functions in a more optimal way across multiple dimensions when these two sys-tems are in harmony.

HRV researchers believe that our ability to effectively reg-ulate emotions depends on our ability to flexibly adjust our physiological response to a changing environment. Having a flexible operating system, both mentally and physically, enables us to roll with the waves of life rather than tensing up, resisting change, and breaking down from stress. Empirical studies have shown that low HRV has been associated with depression, anxi-ety, and cardiovascular disease, while higher HRV is found in people with effective coping strategies and attention control. Having a structured process to monitor HRV makes practice easier, enables you to track progress as you train, and provides a fun and motivating game-like experience.

Anytime you tune into present-moment sensations in the body, you automatically shift mental activity to different parts of the brain. Examples of this include the recharge process we discussed earlier along with other forms of mindfulness, medi-tation, and relaxation. Activities that help stimulate the often-neglected areas of the brain include those that incorporate art, music, and other creative endeavors. If we are to train our brains to be more versatile, flexible, and resilient, we must ul-timately be able to shift out of thinking and problem-solving mode and into reflective, insight mode. Of course, this re-quires that we set aside time and mental space to practice our ability to do nothing at all.

SHARP Science: Laughter Really Is the Best Medicine

Laughter provides benefits across multiple dimensions: emotional, mental, spiritual, and physical. Research conducted at the University of Maryland School of Medicine showed that watching a funny movie or sitcom that produces laughter has a positive effect on vascular function (blood flow), opposite to that observed after watching a movie that causes a stressful response. When study participants watched a stressful movie, their body responded with vasoconstriction, a reduction of blood flow. However, after watching a funny movie, the endothelium (blood vessel lining) expanded, allowing for freer blood flow. According to lead researcher Dr. Miller, the magnitude of change detected in the endothelium was similar to what we could expect to see with aerobic exercise or medication use.[10]

Cultivate Creativity

Do you ever notice that your best ideas usually come when you're not actively *trying* to be creative or solve a problem? When you give yourself the opportunity and space to quiet your mind, you allow your brain to be more flexible to think outside the box. It therefore becomes easier to connect multiple perspectives, which frequently leads to a new and improved solution.

A few years ago I decided to commit to getting a weekly massage in order to manage my stress levels. Although I initially made this investment in order to decrease stress hormones so I would be healthier, I discovered that it was the best investment I could ever make for my *business*, believe it or not. This is because all of my best ideas have come to me during a massage. My intention during this time is to quiet my mind and relax my body, and I used to have a very difficult time turning my brain off. I couldn't quite shift out of thinking and really focus on simply relaxing my muscles. I found that being actively involved in the relaxation process was important for me; otherwise, I would just tense up during the experience and not get the relaxation results I longed for.

I occasionally become too focused on my work, and so I look forward to massage in order to help me with my writing. I often feel my stress levels growing when I strive to be creative, since I become increasingly stumped for new ideas. However, when I concentrate on quieting my mind and relaxing my body, without judging myself or my thoughts, *that's* when I discover new solutions, fresh ideas, and a boost in my creativity. I believe in this concept so much I even made it company policy that all members of our team get monthly massage (or other spa service) every month—my treat!

When I first started what I now call *strategic massage*, I had to keep a notebook nearby because I was so concerned that I would forget the important insights that hit me. As I have practiced and become more secure in the process, I've been able to actually quiet my mind and let thoughts go. I am confident that anything significant will still be in my brain's memory for me when I need it.

I still keep a notebook in my bag so I can spend a few minutes post-massage jotting down any ideas that I've held onto. However, the most crucial element is that I don't fight myself between relaxation and trying to hold onto those thoughts during the process. Even if I can't immediately remember my new thoughts and observations, I have faith that my brain will properly store those ideas and remind me of them in the future, especially if I am consistent with my recharge practice during the day, and throughout the week. (By the way, I'm actually writing this section during a recharge break!)

SHARP Science: Massage Inflammation Away

If you've ever experienced massage, you know it makes you feel good by enhancing circulation and relaxing muscles. Studies now support the benefits of massage at a cellular level—namely, reducing inflammation and stimulating the growth of new mitochondria (the energy-producing parts of a cell) in skeletal muscle. Scientists at California's Buck Institute for Research on Aging analyzed biopsied tissue samples, comparing leg muscle prior to exercise, immediately after 10 minutes of massage treatment, and after a 2.5-hour recovery period. Massage decreased the expression of inflammatory cytokines and promoted the growth of new mitochondria in the muscle cells. This finding provides evidence that massage therapy may be a justifiable part of healing practices for a broad spectrum of individuals including the elderly, those suffering from injuries, or people struggling with inflammatory disease. Considering the impact of inflammation on most diseases of the body and brain, massage would likely be beneficial as a preventive measure as well.[11]

What strategy do you use when you want to be creative or solve a problem? What go-to activity do you know will help fuel the energy demands of a more creative brain?

When you know of upcoming demands on your system, like a need for focused concentration or a desire to think outside the box, think of a brain recharge or other energy-boosting activity as an *investment* in the future. It might sound a bit crazy, but consider it to be similar to going shopping or even on vacation. Since those activities usually require more money than you usually spend, the commonsense approach would be to save up so that you can relax and enjoy yourself. Having a brain that is energized will allow you to dive into tasks, projects, meetings, presentations, and other engagements, knowing that you're fully charged and ready to give it your all.

Training Tips:
- Attention requires energy.
- Oscillation (taking regular mental breaks) helps focus attention.
- Mindfulness matters.
- We have a negativity bias.
- You can make over your mindset.

Training Techniques:
- Each morning, chunk your day into time blocks during which you can fully focus on one task at a time.
- Schedule 50- or 55-minute hours so you have time in between appointments to relax, reflect, and prepare for your next meeting.
- Do distraction resistance and focusing exercises.
- Practice visualization.
- Utilize biofeedback for to control your attention.
- Play concentration games online. (See www.synergyprograms .com/braingym for examples.)

- Complete challenging puzzles and brain teasers.
- Schedule time for reflection and creativity regularly throughout the day.
- Write down three things you're grateful for each morning.
- Send a thank-you card to someone you appreciate each week.

Training Exercise #4: Build Gratitude

One of the easiest ways to create a more optimistic mindset is to take note of the good things happening in your life. So, try it for yourself. Commit to start a gratitude journal, and plan to write down three things you're grateful for each day. These don't have to be life-changing events— sometimes recognizing the simplest things in life has an even greater impact, as we tend to miss out on feeling grateful for the small stuff. For optimal benefit, share your gratitude list with a friend, family member, or accountability group. Keep in mind that sharing what you're grateful for in life has a twofold positive effect: You boost your own sense of appreciation and happiness, *and* you remind others to pause and reflect on what's good in their own lives. Gratitude is contagious, so spread the good word!

What are three things you're grateful for right now?

1. _____

2. _____

3. _____

5

Energize Your Body

One of the brain's most critical responsibilities is to make sure that we meet the energy requirements necessary to keep our systems running. We create energy in the body with two key components: glucose and oxygen.

Phase Four of the SHARP Solution will focus on techniques that help you activate your physical energy by nourishing your body and brain through a variety of methods. We'll focus on the need for good nutrition, eating mindfully, moving more frequently throughout the day, exercising strategically, and prioritizing rest and sleep. This will activate your physical energy source in order to provide the fuel you need to be at your best, while also keeping blood sugar levels stable to ensure the brain that you have consistent energy and don't need to conserve resources.

The brain's primary responsibility is to keep us alive, which requires an adequate amount of energy to fuel the cells of our body. In order to keep our brain functioning at its best, we have to keep glucose and oxygen levels steady throughout the day. Maintaining optimal circulation in the body and brain not only maintains our energy levels; it also balances mood, improves concentration, reduces fatigue, decreases cravings, and stabilizes stress hormones.

As we discussed earlier, sometimes the CEO and the CFO—the heart and brain, respectively—don't agree on the most important goals in the moment. There are times when we want to take a certain action or perform a task with all of our heart. However, if our brain perceives that we are in an energy shortage, it will put our system into conservation mode. This means that even though we *want* to or believe we *should* do something, our brains often talk us out of it.

Exercise is a perfect example of this. When we are worn out from the demands of the day, we may think that we *should* exercise; however, the brain perceives this as another demand for energy—one that it can't take on when it's already exhausted. Without much thought, we decide that exercising *tomorrow* would be in our best interest.

If we ask for more energy than we have in the moment, the brain will give us a million reasons why it's not a good idea. It'll remind us that we've tried this before and it didn't work, we're tired and it's better for us to rest, or we'll just start tomorrow. Doing it *tomorrow* always sounds like a better idea to a tired brain because it knows that expending energy will be a more feasible option after a good night's sleep. We obviously know that's not always the case, (snooze button), but the brain's argument still usually wins nonetheless. The problem is that there's always another *tomorrow* that seems better than *today*.

Fortunately, you can use some simple energy management techniques to create a solid foundation of glucose and oxygen management to keep the brain and body adequately fueled throughout the day. And these don't have to include going on a diet or becoming a gym rat. In fact, the stress created by crash dieting or excessive exercise often creates an increase in unhealthy cortisol in the system, thereby canceling out any benefits you *should* get by making good choices. Usually, when we experience strong cravings for food—especially sugar—we're really just seeking a quick energy boost. You may find that doing a short brain recharge to invest in your brain and body is enough to make your cravings go away as you restore your natural energy balance.

alzheim

It's equally important not to *worry* about how to fuel your brain and body, considering the resulting stress is exactly what we need to eliminate to keep our system functioning at its best. It's better to focus on developing an optimal brain diet by adding each of the following steps, one at a time:

1. Balance blood sugar.
2. Optimize blood flow.
3. Prioritize rest and recovery.

These three key strategies to nourishing your body will optimize your brain. Let's discuss each one in further detail.

Balance Blood Sugar

One of the most important ways to maintain your brain's health and performance is to keep blood sugar levels stable throughout the day. The problem is that our current lifestyle seems to support exactly the opposite of what our brain craves: consistency. We're usually rushing through our days, sometimes completely unaware of hunger due to constant stress and busyness. The fact is that eating just once or twice a day not only wreaks havoc on your energy levels; it's also certain to expand your waistline. As if that's not enough, sugar spikes throughout the day have been shown to be toxic to the brain.

According to a series of interviews by Alvaro Fernandez and Dr. Elkhonon Goldberg published in *The Sharp Brains Guide to Brain Fitness*, a lack of glucose causes us to be starved of energy, while too much can overload the body and brain. Scientific studies show that insulin spikes may be damaging to brain cells, which could be why some brain experts consider Alzheimer's disease to be "Type 3 diabetes."[1]

Scientists believe that brain insulin resistance maybe be an important contributor to the cognitive decline associated with Alzheimer's disease. The risk of developing Alzheimer's disease increases by 50 percent in people with diabetes. A recent study analyzed brain tissue from non-diabetic Alzheimer's patients and noticed less insulin activation compared to tissue from people who had died from other causes.[2] Studies evaluating potential medications that target brain insulin resistance are currently being conducted.

SHARP Science: Brain Drain

A recent study out of UCLA showed that eating a high-fructose diet could alter your brain's ability to learn and remember information. According to researchers, having a diet high in DHA, an omega-3 fatty acid, helps to protect the brain from damage by strengthening neural connections. The scientists suspect that eating too much fructose could block insulin's ability to regulate how cells use and store the sugar required to process thoughts and emotions. There is no need to deprive yourself of things you like, but when possible swap sugary sweets and snacks for more balanced versions such as Greek yogurt, fresh berries, or nuts. To boost protective DHA levels in the brain, try to eat foods rich in omgea-3 fatty acids such as salmon, walnuts, and flaxseeds, or consider taking 1 gram of DHA per day.[3]

We meet our optimal blood-sugar balance when we combine adequate protein—a slow releasing energy source—with a quicker source of energy like a complex carbohydrate. Because every person is unique, we all have a different optimal nutrition balance, so one size doesn't fit all when it comes to meal planning. However, there are some general guidelines most people can follow in order to stabilize blood sugar, optimize blood flow, and provide the most beneficial nutrients to the brain.

Most brains benefit from a plate that looks something like the picture below, which is based on a Mediterranean diet approach. I recommend the Mediterranean diet because it includes a nice balance of complex carbohydrates, lean protein, and healthy fat with primarily plant-based foods, which have been shown to decrease the risk of all modern diseases. Not only will this optimize your energy while helping you maintain a healthy weight, but you will also be providing your brain with powerful nutrients that have been shown to reduce the risk of dementia. A study of 2,000 Manhattan residents averaging 76 years of age found that those eating a Mediterranean diet had a 68 percent lower risk of developing Alzheimer's disease.[4]

This distribution of 50 percent fruits and vegetables, 25 percent lean protein, and 25 percent complex carbohydrates should keep blood-sugar levels steady while providing essential nutrients for energy production. Aim to fill your plate with clean, natural foods as often as possible. A food is considered to be "clean" when it doesn't have additives or preservatives, and has not been processed. You want the majority of your food to come from plant sources, as they're rich in health-promoting antioxidants, phytochemicals, vitamins, minerals, and fiber.

SHARP Science: A Berry Healthy Brain

A recent review in the *Journal of Agricultural and Food Chemistry* concluded that berries help keep the brain healthy in several ways. Blueberries, blackberries, and strawberries especially contain high levels of antioxidants, compounds that protect cells from damage by free radicals. Berries also appear to change the way the brain communicates by preventing brain inflammation, which improves cognitive functioning.[5]

Maximize Your Return on Investment

Once you have balanced blood sugar levels throughout the day, you can then choose to maximize your return on investment (ROI) by eating foods that provide a high nutrient value with little cost. You're already optimizing your fuel source by focusing on natural foods; however, this strategy can also help you make good decisions when things seem a little more complicated. It would be lovely if we were able to grow our own food organically in our backyards, but the reality is that most of us can't. And considering how busy our lifestyles have become, we must be realistic about the nutrition plan we put together.

I find it fairly easy to eat clean when I'm home because I can control how my food is prepared by making it myself, but my choices on the road are much more limited. I quickly realized when my travel schedule became chaotic that I needed to create some simple guidelines to make the best possible choices in a range of situations. When you think about your options, it may be helpful to consider the following equation:

$$\text{Fuel value} = \text{Benefits} - \text{Costs.}$$

Keep in mind, the benefits don't only include the actual nutrients a food provides, but also how much we *enjoy* that food. If I have a high-value food that is also one I really like, then having a few costs might not be that big a deal. Costs are food characteristics that can have a negative impact on your physical, mental, or emotional energy (e.g., high fat or calorie content, somewhat processed, artificially sweetened, etc).

If you are able to eat clean, high-value foods 90 percent of the time, I guarantee you that you won't notice the negative effects of indulging in the lower-value foods that you enjoy 10 percent of the time. This strategy can also help you lose weight without feeling deprived, which is a goal for many people. Of course, you may choose to ignore this 90/10 rule sometimes for special occasions, but as long as you stay on track most of the time, you won't experience any lasting side effects of overindulgence.

It never ceases to amaze me how much we use an item's monetary value to determine its worth. For example, fast food restaurants tout their –"Value Meals"—which provide a ridiculous amount of low- or no-quality food for a very low price—as a great deal. You can pay a small fee for entry into a buffet line that promises an endless array of delicious, home-style comfort foods, but in reality, you're handing over your hard earned money for a smorgasbord of non-perishable food products laid out like a trough—one that allows you to pile up your plate repeatedly and top it off with an overly full, self-serve ice cream sundae.

Let me ask you: Have you ever tried to eat as little as possible all day long because you're planning to eat a ton of food later at a restaurant or party? You're likely trying to save room in your stomach so you can maximize your investment, but did you ever consider that the investment you were maximizing was situated around your waistline? I cringe when I hear parents encouraging their kids to "get their fill while they can," so they can get their money's worth. Because what is that money really buying them, other than a gut ache, sluggish body, cloudy thinking, and a food coma on the couch when they get home?

If this sounds familiar, you might consider changing your mental script. When you think about the *value* of food, shift the message away from how much *volume* you can get for a dollar to how much *nutritional value* you can get for your calories. For example, if you look at the price per calorie of a box of doughnuts you'll find it to be quite inexpensive. You get much more quality fuel from a handful of organic blueberries. Although they may cost more per calorie, they are chock-full of beneficial nutrients such as vitamins, minerals, antioxidants, phytochemicals, fiber, and more. The true *value* of healthy food means you're getting way more for your money, and you can train your brain to look at things this way. Once you do, you'll be more apt to spend a little bit more on higher-quality produce, grass-fed beef, free-range poultry, organic dairy products and eggs, nutrient-rich nuts and seeds, and so on. You might even recognize that it's a worthy investment to pay a bit extra for a service that provides pre-made organic meals portioned appropriately. We just have to be able to think about it the right way, and not get caught up in what the media is trying to convince us: that *more volume* is what matters. But of course, just understanding this new view of food value won't make it easy to *apply* it.

SHARP Science: Neural Nutrients

A recent study published in the journal *Neuron* suggests that there is a different cellular response to different types of diets. The response of specific neurons that regulate energy balance in the body (orexin/hypocretin neurons) varies depending on nutrient type. Based on behavior observed in the study, protein rich meals are more effective at promoting wakefulness and arousal than sugar-rich meals.[6]

Remember: Your brain's primary responsibility is to get energy to fuel the body. Excess calories are therefore considered a bonus when it comes to securing our long-term survival. It's important to re-train our ourselves about the value of food, as well as the appropriate portion size for our body. This way, our calorie-greedy brain can't continue to fool us. If you struggle with portion sizes, as most people do, I highly recommend you take some time to train your brain to recognize how much food you *actually need* by being mindful about your serving sizes.

This doesn't mean you have to literally measure or weigh your food, though some people do. It's a good general rule to take less than you think you need. Try eating half of what you usually do. You might be shocked to find out that you actually feel more energized with *fewer* calories. You can use your own hand as a guideline for the amount of food that's right for you. Most people do well with a one-handful serving of complex carbohydrates, one palm-size serving of lean protein, and two handfuls of fruit and/or vegetables at each meal.

Balanced snacks of about 100–150 calories with some protein, fat, and fiber, in addition to carbohydrates will most likely provide you with about two hours of energy. Foods with a balance of nutrients are considered low-glycemic because they provide a steadier source of glucose, while foods that are highly processed or consist only of carbohydrates will spike glucose. High-glycemic foods no only put you on an energy roller-coaster, but they may also spike insulin production and inflammatory agents that can be damaging to both the body and the brain. Some nutrient-rich, low-glycemic snack options include:

- Peanut or almond butter and whole-grain crackers
- Hummus and pita bread
- An apple, orange, pear, or bowl of berries
- Greek yogurt, low-fat cheese, or cottage cheese with fruit
- Almonds, pistachios, cashews, walnuts, and pecans
- A small glass of almond or soy milk
- Half of an all-natural nutrition bar
- A small latte
- Steamed edamame
- Trail mix

Keep in mind that your brain will tend to resist change if it perceives the effort to be too great. When blood sugar is low, the brain recognizes an energy shortage and will compensate by slowing down metabolism to put the system into conservation mode. This limits the amount of energy that you can spend on non-essential functions such as changing behavior or connecting to a deeper sense of purpose. Therefore, establishing a consistent fueling routine is one of the most fundamental ways to convince the brain that it has enough. This will both support optimal functioning and provide the energy you need to make good choices.

Be Prepared

One of the keys to a worry-free diet is being prepared for anything. We've all experienced days, or maybe even weeks, where we started off with the best of intentions but something pulled us off course.

There will always be unexpected bumps in the road, which is why it's so important to be prepared for challenges and obstacles before they happen. This may take a bit of extra time up front, but as you train yourself to make preparation a habit, you'll quickly find that it becomes part of your automatic morning or evening routine.

So that you don't find yourself stuck and starting to worry, use my three Ps: *plan*, *prepare*, and *pack*.

First, choose one day a week to spend a few minutes thinking through your upcoming weekly schedule; be especially aware of any particular situations or events that might require a bit more preparation. For example, a company function in the evening will be full of temptations; so consider what you could eat as a snack beforehand to make sure you're not going to the event hungry (a small bowl of soup, some leafy greens or a small handful of almonds are good options).

Additionally, you might not have time to stop for a healthy lunch if you have to drive all day long from meeting to meeting. Come up with some ideas for food you can keep in the car that won't spoil or melt like a half sandwich, or an apple and some almonds. You can also think about a good place on your route to stop for a quick but healthy meal.

You should probably assume you won't get anything healthy on your flight if you're traveling by plane, so determine what you can bring with you or decide ahead of time what snacks you will buy at the airport market. You might be surprised to see what good choices they offer these days. If you can check in a little bit early, you'll be able to decrease your stress levels and explore the healthiest options.

Once you've thought through your plan for the week, determine if you want to do all of your preparation once, or break the week up into a couple of days at a time. Make sure that you schedule in prep time as needed and commit to making it a priority. You may also want to cook a large meal one day a week that can be portioned into small containers and kept in the refrigerator or freezer for easy dining when you're tired and don't feel like making anything.

Finally, be sure to pack your meals and snacks each evening, or make them easy to throw together in the morning. Always have food with you; you never can tell when you're going to find yourself running late to an appointment, sitting too long in a meeting, or stuck in traffic. In fact, you might as well assume at least one of those will happen each day, so plan, prepare, and pack for it ahead of time. Then you won't worry when it does!

Optimize Blood Flow

It may surprise you to hear that exercise can actually be *un-healthy*—and may even make you fatter. That's because, as far as the brain is concerned, you're not exercising because you *want* to; you're doing it because you *have* to. Think about it: Why would you want to expend precious energy exerting yourself unless it was crucial for your survival? While we recognize the importance of fitness in connection to health and longevity nowadays, this is actually a fairly new phenomenon—one that our brains are still getting used to.

In the 1960's a new fad emerged thanks to pioneers such as health and fitness expert Jack LaLanne, but it wasn't that we just suddenly realized exercise was important. Our society had evolved into one that relied more on technology to do the manual labor that humans once performed. We moved out of the fields and into the office, and our active lifestyle became sedentary. When we stopped engaging in physical activities for our daily work routine, our health began to suffer the consequences.

Therefore, purposeful exercise became a way to replace large amounts of day-to-day activity. Instead of exerting energy all day long at work, we spent dedicated segments of time working out. Gyms, health clubs, and spas popped up all over the world as people recognized the unique health benefits and body shaping that exercise could provide.

However, even as people began to consider adding exercise routines, our lives became more and more hectic—and more and more sedentary. The demands on our time continued to grow, along with our waistlines.

Even with stacks of evidence that physical fitness can make you happier, add years to your life, improve self-esteem, enhance mental performance, boost moods, help you sleep—I could go on and on here—people still have a difficult time making exercise a priority. And despite all the people we think we see going to the gym, only about 15 percent of people even get the *minimum* amounts of exercise recommended for good health.

SHARP Science: Train Your Brain and Your Body

According to a Mayo Clinic study, combining mentally and physically stimulating activities decreases your odds of having memory loss more than computer use or exercise alone. The study examined moderate exercise—such as brisk walking, hiking, aerobics, strength training, golfing without a cart, swimming, tennis, yoga, and martial arts—along with mentally stimulating activities such as computer use, playing games, artistic activities, and watching less television. Researchers suggest that there is a synergistic effect between computer use and moderate exercise in protecting brain function in people over the age of 70.[7]

Human beings were built to move. It is estimated that our Paleolithic ancestors had to walk 5 to 10 miles on an average day just to be able to find food and shelter. Our bodies are therefore genetically predisposed to frequent, consistent, whole-body movement, but in modern times, we have reduced this movement to dangerously low levels. Regular physical activity is a crucial part of our daily routine, because it has been shown to:

- Increase breathing and heart rate, which enhances blood flow, energy production, and waste removal.
- Stimulate the release of brain-derived neurotrophic factor, which supports the growth of new neurons.
- Increase the amount and capacity of blood vessels in the brain.
- Boost serotonin, a neurotransmitter that fights depression.
- Normalize sleep patterns.
- Improve self-efficacy and sense of accomplishment.
- Enhance resilience to stress over time.

Remember: Our ancient survival instincts that were so valuable thousands of years ago, continue to steer us to conserve energy—specifically, by eating more and moving less. In order to make physical activity something we embrace rather than avoid in these modern times, we must consciously train our brain to perceive movement as a daily benefit that's worth the upfront energy investment.

The solution is therefore *not* to jump into an intense workout regimen right away. You can minimize the stress response in your body and brain by first easing into more consistent daily activity that you just add to your current routine. This will keep your brain from seeing the movement as such a huge upfront investment, and your mind won't try so hard to talk you out of it.

One way to make it easier to incorporate physical activity into your already-busy schedule is to gradually increase the general movement you get throughout the day. This may actually be more important to health and weight loss than the purposeful exercise we get in the gym, since it turns out that the longer people sit, the higher their risk of many health problems, regardless of the amount of exercise they do. A study published in the *American Journal of Epidemiology* showed that among 123,000 adults followed over 14 years, those who sat more than six hours a day were at least 18 percent more likely to die than those who sat less than three hours a day.[8]

If you were to look at your total caloric expenditure over the course of the day you'd find that only a small amount comes from purposeful exercise. The vast majority comes from the energy required just for our body and brain to operate our system effectively through what's known as our *resting metabolic rate* (RMR). In addition to RMR, we also expend energy on non-exercise activities that just happen as part of the day-to-day routine: our non-exercise activity thermogenesis, otherwise known as NEAT.

The Mayo Clinic conducted a study that evaluated the difference in caloric expenditure in a group of non-exercisers (self-proclaimed couch potatoes) to identify differences between lean and obese individuals. While sleep times were equal for both groups, they found that the obese group sat for 164 minutes longer than the lean group, adding up to a difference in energy expenditure of about 350 calories a day.[9] This is enough to add approximately 35 pounds in one year! (Keep in mind that research has demonstrated that NEAT can vary by 2,000 calories a day.)

Simply *standing* instead of sitting can double metabolism, and walking can multiply resting metabolism fivefold. Consider the following strategies to maximize your NEAT:

- Modify behaviors that are usually seated by making rules to stand at certain times, like when watching television or reading.
- Use a headset and walk around while talking for calls longer than a few minutes.
- Utilize a standing desk or countertop for work.
- Allow sedentary behavior only after accumulating time with activity. For example, you can play computer or video games after walking for 30 minutes or climbing stairs for 10.
- Start slowly by adding 5–10 minutes every day for a week, with a goal of an extra 1–2 hours of accumulated general activity each day.
- Use self-monitoring devices such as pedometers or calorie measuring applications (such as Fitbit, NikeFuel, or BodyBug) to track progress and boost accountability.

Not only is NEAT easy to do and highly effective, but because there is no reason for the brain to engage the stress response system, it is also not stressful to the body; enabling your system to function on all cylinders.

As you begin to increase the time you spend moving, you can slowly add activities that will challenge you even more, thereby boosting your fitness levels and creating a more effective operating system (and fat burning system, if you so desire). In order to actually burn more calories, we have to keep our heart and lungs functioning optimally and increase—or at least maintain—our muscle mass. It's important to remember, however, that dragging yourself through countless boring workouts at the gym is most likely *not* going to be a good long-term strategy.

To recap, here are three suggestions for making physical activity more enjoyable, so that you can make it a part of your life for good:

1. Ease into movement (take small steps that are non-stressful and gentle).
2. Find activities that are fun, enjoyable, and positive while simple to maintain without excess equipment or expensive memberships (e.g., walking/jogging outdoors, dancing, interactive video games).
3. Make fitness social to help with accountability and the fun factor (e.g., partner with a workout buddy, play on a sports team, or join a club).

SHARP Science: Team-Up for a Better Workout

A new study shows that a being part of a team may increase motivation and compliance to exercise. Researchers at Michigan State University placed 58 women in one of three groups: The first who exercised independently with a virtual partner, the second who competed in teams with a virtual partner, and the control group who cycled alone. Those who cycled in a team exercised an average of two minutes longer than those who exercised independently with a virtual partner, and twice as long as those without a partner.[10]

Prioritize Rest and Recovery

According to the National Sleep Foundation, approximately 70 million Americans are affected by chronic sleep loss or sleep disorders. The annual costs associated with sleep deprivation are estimated at $16 billion in health care expenses and $50 billion in lost productivity.[11]

Sleep deprivation and sleepiness have adverse effects on performance, response times, accuracy, attention, and concentration. Lack of quality sleep has been associated with a wide range of quality-of-life measures, such as social functioning, mental and physical health – even early death.[12] It's also been correlated with obesity, increases in smoking and alcohol use, inactivity, inflammation and heart disease, and blood sugar imbalances. A lack of sleep puts your body under additional stress, which may trigger an increase of adrenaline, cortisol, and other stress hormones during the day. A recent study found that men who only had four hours of sleep for two consecutive nights experienced hormonal changes that made them feel hungry and crave carbohydrate-rich foods such as cakes, candy, ice cream, and pasta.[13] Your body is not able to undergo the proper recovery cycles when you fail to get adequate sleep. This means that you miss the opportunity for your blood pressure to dip during the evening. This may negatively impact your heart and vascular system by increasing C-reactive protein (CRP), released when there is inflammation in the body), which has been shown to increase the risk of developing heart disease. Immune functioning is also compromised by too little sleep, because we fail to produce the necessary hormones and other molecules we need to fight off infection.

Sleep is not just about giving our system a rest. It is also the time when our body and brain do some of their most important work repairing and rebuilding muscle tissue and strengthening neural connections that improve learning and memory. The area of the brain that may be most affected by sleep, or the lack of it, is the prefrontal cortex, responsible for executive functioning processes such as learning, judgment, reasoning, memory consolidation, and understanding. According to a study by the Better Sleep Council, sleep deprivation impairs the quality and accuracy of work (31 percent), clear thinking and judgment (31 percent), and memory of important details (30 percent).[14] Studies performed with both animals and humans suggest that brain activity that occurs during the day is reactivated during sleep as your brain consolidates memory. Just like the muscles in our body, the pathways in our brain require rest to, repair, rebuild, and form stronger connections.

SHARP Science: Sleep More, Stress Less

A lack of sleep may limit the body's natural ability to heal itself. In a study at the University of Rochester Medical Center, older adults who slept poorly showed a heightened inflammatory response to acute stress, as reflected in an increase of interleukin-6 (IL-6), a protein primarily produced at sites of inflammation. Poor sleepers also reported more depressive symptoms, loneliness, and perceived stress relative to good sleepers.[15]

Numerous studies have shown the detrimental impact that sleep deprivation has on performance and health. According to the National Institutes of Health, sleeping less than 6 hours in a given night can seriously hinder a person's ability to think and act properly, even when you feel that you're functioning just fine. A University of Pennsylvania study found that subjects who slept 4 to 6 hours a night for 14 consecutive nights showed deficits in cognitive performance equivalent to how they would perform after going without sleep for up to three days in a row.[16]

How Much Sleep Do We Really Need?

The optimal amount of sleep is unique to each individual. To determine how much sleep you need, you have to find out how much time it takes for you to wake up feeling refreshed *without* needing an alarm clock. Studies show that humans need 6 to 10 hours of sleep each night, which is why you've most likely heard the recommendation for an average of 8 hours each night.

However, some people can function well with 6 hours of sleep while other people need all 10. According to recent research, dipping below the six-hour mark impairs cognitive functioning and increases symptoms of stress for just about everyone, so it is recommended that you always get *at least* six hours of quality sleep each night.

SHARP Science: Sleep Your Cravings Away

Brain scans show that our desire for junk food increases when we are sleep-deprived. Many studies have shown an increase in overall food consumption, most likely in a response to an energy-deficit. Using fMRI scans, researchers

---

from New York's St. Luke's Roosevelt Hospital Center and Columbia University detected higher activity in reward centers in the sleep-deprived brains that were less active when participants had adequate sleep, proving a neurological basis to the quest for high-calorie, high-fat food.[17]

How do you know if you're not getting enough sleep? If any of the following apply to you, you probably need to get more shut-eye:

- **You're dependent on an alarm clock.** If you're getting enough sleep, you should be able to wake up on time *without* a morning alarm.
- **You're driving drowsy.** Falling asleep at the wheel is a sure sign that you are too tired. It's also incredibly dangerous, as drowsy driving is a common cause of deadly auto accidents.
- **You're attached to the coffee pot.** It's fine to start with a cup of coffee, but you shouldn't have to rely on coffee (or other energy drinks) to stay awake throughout the *entire* day.
- **You're making a lot of mistakes.** It's harder to focus and concentrate when you are tired. You're more easily distracted and less likely to catch and fix errors.
- **You're forgetful.** Sleep loss may explain why you have a hard time remembering things, since sleep deprivation hinders short-term memory.
- **You're snippy and irritable.** Being tired can have a negative effect on your moods. It makes you more likely to feel depressed, anxious, and frustrated.

- **You're frequently sick.** Your immune system is not at full strength without sleep, thereby making it harder for your body to fight illness.

Oscillation Improves Sleep

I have mentioned in previous chapters how crucial oscillation—taking breaks throughout the day—is to the human system, both mentally and physically. Instead of thinking of our day as one long marathon, we're better off if we divide it up into smaller sprints. This allows us to both concentrate on our tasks *and* get the strategic breaks we need to improve our ability to recover more effectively and efficiently. Incorporating relaxation strategies throughout the day also helps us keep stress levels down so we aren't trying to fall asleep after a constant rush of adrenaline. We can't go at light speed all day long and expect our system to come to a screeching halt once we crawl into bed.

It always surprises me when my clients don't understand why they feel tired or aren't sleeping well. The first question I always ask: "Do you take breaks during the day?" While it may seem like this has nothing to do with sleep, it is actually one of the most important factors.

Even if you utilize healthy sleep rituals, limit caffeine, and turn off distractions, your brain can't immediately shut down just because you tell it to after you have been going at a hectic pace all day.

Have you ever tried to read a book before bed? If you're like most people, you only make it through a few pages before starting to feel sleepy. There are several reasons why reading helps to induce sleep. For one thing, it takes your mind off the worries or stress of the day, and it may provide relaxation through entertainment, but the driving force behind this phenomenon is the brain training that occurs as a result of repeatedly connecting a place (bed), an activity (reading), and a desired outcome (falling asleep).

We could derive similar results with other strategies that utilize the same principles of being mentally calming and physically relaxing. For example, if you regularly listen to music before bed, you can practice focusing your mind on relaxation. Including a warm bath provides extra benefit as your body's natural cooling-down process can enhance sleep.

Whatever mind-calming, relaxing activity you choose to do at bedtime—listening to music, taking a bath, reading a book, drinking warm milk, going for a walk—the more you associate that behavior with sleep, the more your brain will begin to anticipate the connection, and the quicker you will find yourself in restful slumber.

Sleep Strategies

While some activities can assist you in falling and staying asleep long enough to feel rested, there are others that need to be avoided before bedtime. Here are a few tips for sleeping well:

- *Go to bed early.* Some studies suggest that early to bed and early to rise is more suited for our natural rhythms.
- *Get out of bed.* If you have trouble falling asleep, get out of bed and do something relaxing until you feel sleepy.
- *Limit naps.* Napping can be helpful to recharge your energy, but be sure to keep them brief. Nap only for less than an hour, and before 3 p.m.

- *Wake up on the weekend.* It is best to go to bed and wake up at the same times on the weekend as you do during the workweek. This enables you to build a steady pattern around your sleep schedule.

- *Avoid late-day caffeine.* Avoid caffeine in the afternoon and at night. It stays in your system for hours and can make it hard for you to fall asleep.

- *Adjust the lights.* Dim the lights in the evening so your body knows it will soon be time to sleep. Let in the sunlight in the morning to boost your alertness.

- *Wind down.* Take some time to wind down before going to bed. Get away from the computer, turn off the TV and your cell phone, and relax quietly for 15–30 minutes. Parents should keep TVs and computers out of their children's bedrooms.

- *Eat a little.* Never eat a large meal right before bedtime. While a big meal may cause you to feel drowsy, your body will have to work hard to process all of that food, which can actually stimulate your system. Enjoy a healthy snack or light dessert (such as a handful of almonds or a small bowl of frozen blueberries with yogurt) so you don't go to bed hungry.

- *Avoid alcohol.* While it seems like a drink or two may help you fall asleep, it may also keep you from getting the *quality* of sleep you need. The body quickly metabolizes alcohol, which has a stimulating effect on the brain. This disrupts sleep, even when you don't wake up.

For more information on sleep, including when you should see a sleep specialist, visit the National Sleep Foundation at www.sleepfoundation.org.

Training Tips:
- Balance blood sugar.
- Optimize blood flow.
- Maximize your nutrient ROI.
- Move frequently.
- Prioritize rest and recovery.

Training Techniques:
- Eat something balanced (carbohydrate and protein) every 3 to 4 hours.
- Plan strategic snacks mid-morning and mid-afternoon.
- Drink water consistently (fill a large jug or container each morning and set a goal to finish it before heading home at the end of the day).
- Get out of your chair and move for at least five minutes every hour.
- Lead a walking group at your office.
- Train for a run or cycling event.
- Go to bed earlier.
- Plan a new bedtime ritual to help you fall asleep.
- Avoid caffeine after noon.
- Get 7 to 8 hours of sleep every night.

Training Exercise #5: Have a NEAT Day

Make today a NEAT day by maximizing your opportunities to boost metabolism through general activity. Use a timer set to alert you every hour, and plan to get up and move for three to five minutes.

The following are suggestions for ways to maximize your NEAT when you take your movement breaks:

- Walk around.
- Go visit a colleague instead of sending an email or text.
- Play with your kids.
- Walk the dog.
- Water the plants.
- Do a few squats next to your chair.
- Time yourself and do a few exercises each lasting about 30 seconds, such as jumping jacks, dips, and lunges.
- Take the stairs when it's an option.
- Work from a standing desk or countertop.
- Go through a short yoga session online or simply move through a few yoga poses.
- Stretch.
- Use a resistance band for strength training.
- Park further away from your building's entrance.
- Avoid the drive-thru and get out of the car.
- Do the dishes.
- Vacuum.
- Make a few calls using a headset and walk while talking.
- Run an errand for a friend.
- Give away your seat on the bus and stand for a while.
- Play an active video game like Wii or Kinect.

Strengthen Your Community

The fifth and final phase of the SHARP Solution will focus on techniques that help you build support by connecting with others, investing in your social capital, creating strategic alliances, setting yourself up for success, and teaching others about what you've learned for added accountability. This phase will strengthen your sense of community, which will in turn boost your social energy source and provide you with extra accountability and support for your journey.

When it comes to our survival instincts, being part of the right crowd may be one of the most important factors keeping us alive. Researchers often trigger the physiological stress response in animals by removing them from their social structure, as the simple act of isolating them activates stress hormones. The same applies to us—loneliness is a threat to human survival.

Considering all of the technological advances we have to keep us connected, you might think we are more social than ever. However, this constant preoccupation with staying connected has actually torn apart the concept of relationships, as we once knew them. We may have more *breadth* in our number of connections, but it's taken a toll on the *depth* of our relationships.

Keep in mind that social connection is based on *how you feel*, not the number of friends you have or whether you're married or single. A recent study at Harvard examined data from more than 309,000 people and found that a lack of strong relationships increased the risk of premature death from all causes by 50 percent—an effect comparable to smoking up to 15 cigarettes a day, and one that had more of a negative impact than obesity and physical inactivity.[1]

In their book, *Loneliness: Human Nature and the Need for Social Connection*, authors John Cacioppo and William Patrick argue that loneliness, like hunger, is an alarm signal that evolved hundreds of thousands of years ago when group cohesion was essential for fighting off attacks. They conducted a study with children and asked them to evaluate bite-sized cookies. Before tasting the cookies, half the children were told that no one wanted to work with them. The other half were told that everyone wanted to work with them, but that they'd still have to work on their own because it would be impossible to work with so many people. Each student was then handed a plate of cookies and told to evaluate them. In the group that was told everyone wanted to work with them, students ate an average of 4.5 cookies, while members of the rejected group ate an average of 9. Cacioppo and Patrick asked, "Is it any wonder we turn to ice cream when we're sitting at home, feeling all alone in the world?"[2]

As research continues to look at the relevance of social connections, a new field of social science has emerged. *Social neuroscience* analyzes the associations between social and neural connections, and determines the impact of our relationships on health and well-being. John Cacioppo and Gary Berntson have been credited with founding the social neuroscience movement. By evaluating brain scans and monitoring physiological responses, Cacioppo and Berntson found that social context—a sense of connection—had an overpowering influence on the brain and the body. In fact, the impact was so intense that they were able to see changes to the genetic expression in white blood cells. Cacioppo's research shows that loneliness can increase blood pressure, stress, depression, anxiety, and cortisol production.

Feeling lonely changes behavior, as well. Studies have connected loneliness with a decrease in exercise, an increase in caloric consumption (especially comfort foods high in processed carbohydrates), and an increase in alcohol and drug consumption (both prescription and illegal).[3] Loneliness also negatively affects immune functioning, impairs sleep, and has recently been correlated to the risk of developing Alzheimer's disease. Unfortunately, loneliness can be a vicious cycle, as it can trigger a sense of sadness that causes even more isolation and an even greater sense of loneliness.

But feeling connected to other people can change us, both physically and mentally, for the better. When we make a positive social connection, our brain releases a feel-good chemical called oxytocin, which instantly reduces anxiety and improves focus and concentration. In 2008, Oscar Ybarra and his colleagues evaluated the social engagement of 3,600 people aged 24 to 96. They found that the more connected people were, the better they performed on a mental exam.[4] Social support also enhances cardiovascular and immune system functioning, whereas lack of social support has been shown to increase blood pressure by 30 points.[5]

SHARP Science: Social Support is Life Support

Loneliness has been linked to both psychological and physiological distress in children and adults. New studies show that older adults who experience loneliness are at higher risk of functional decline and death, according to a report in the *Archives of Internal Medicine*. Of the 1,604 participants in a Health and Retirement Study conducted by the National Institute on Aging, 43.2 percent reported feeling lonely, which was associated with an increased risk of death over the six-year follow-up period. Loneliness was also linked to a decrease in functional abilities, including a decline in activities of daily living and difficulties with upper extremity tasks and stair climbing.[6]

Connection not only helps our health and performance when we're feeling well, it also boosts our ability to recover when we're sick or injured. People who receive support during the healing process are shown to have improved chances of recovery. For example, heart attack survivors were three times more likely to survive when they received social support and breast cancer patients who participated in a breast cancer support group doubled life expectancy post-surgery.[7,8] In other words, the amount of stress we feel about something challenging is lessened when we are with people we care about and when we feel cared for. The benefits of social support extend to healthy people, too. A study of perception revealed that participants who were accompanied by a friend estimated a hill to be less steep than those who were alone.[9]

Connection also increases our sense of purpose. Feeling linked to other people directly correlates with our having a sense of meaning in life. Just think about it: Very few of our most positive moments in life happen in isolation. Consider the last time you laughed so hard that you cried, or were overwhelmed with feelings of joy. How about the last time you felt incredibly proud of an accomplishment? Most likely, you weren't alone. Experts agree that relationships may be the most important contributor to overall life satisfaction and emotional well-being among people of all ages and cultures.

Connection Is Based on Perception

Although relationships are incredibly enriching, being alone doesn't have to be lonely, which is a good thing, considering how many of us are on our own. The latest Census figures indicate there are some 31 million Americans living alone, which accounts for more than a quarter of all U.S. households. As with having strong relationships, there are of course many benefits to being on your own. Quality time in solitude can help us to unwind and recharge so that we have more energy to give to the people around us. Some studies also highlight the benefit of isolation for certain cognitive functions, such as memory (concentrating more when we think we're alone), empathy (taking time to think through how others may feel), focus (decreasing multitasking), and judgment (not being influenced by other's perspectives).

Keep in mind that how we feel is completely based on *our perception* of what's going on, not the specifics regarding how often we are social, whether we are single or married, or the number of friends we have. The negative consequences of loneliness most likely have more to do with the anxiety or depression that can result from feeling alone rather than the actual state of being by yourself.

While staying connected is definitely an important part of overall health and wellness, working on your perception can also decrease your sense of loneliness at times when you may not be as connected as you would like. We've already discussed strategies for shifting your mindset, and this might be a good opportunity to practice if you're feeling disconnected.

Quantity versus Quality

The problem with being overly connected—as you may have realized if you're an active social networker—is that it's impossible to maintain the same depth of connection with so many people. Take social networking site Facebook as an example. Many of my friends brag about the number of "friends" they've amassed on this platform. But ask them what is currently going on in any one of these individual's lives, and they'll most likely look at you like you're crazy (and then un-friend you).

Social networking websites and tools are great for expanding your quantity of connections. However, you quickly realize how impossible it is to keep up with what every single friend is doing. Staying on top of hundreds of new posts each day would require a full-time commitment. That said, I still use Facebook myself; I find it very valuable when I'm conducting a survey, trying to find a good restaurant in a town I'm visiting, or looking to vent about my travel schedule (thanks, FB friends, for listening). But when it comes to feeling connected, or avoiding loneliness, social networking sites just don't seem to cut it for most people.

The fact is that the *quality* of our relationships matters much more than the quantity. Someone with two or three very close friends may feel more fully engaged socially than someone with 20 acquaintances (or 300 Facebook connections). And while marriage was once thought to help people feel connected, it turns out that it's the quality of the relationship (no surprise here), not merely marital status that determines the potential benefit.

SHARP Science: Need a Little Help from My Friends

Children who have a best friend present during a negative experience show stronger levels of self-worth and lower levels of the stress hormone cortisol, according to a study published in the journal *Developmental Psychology*. This can have a lasting impact on development, as high cortisol levels have been shown to suppress immune function and decrease bone formation in children. This study builds upon previous research that shows that friendships can buffer negative social experiences such as bullying and exclusion.[10]

Building Better Relationships

One of the best ways to strengthen existing relationships is to dedicate focused time to people we care about. My clients often complain that they don't have nearly enough time to spend with the people they love. I like to remind them that it's not necessarily about the amount of time we are able to share, but the quality of the energy we bring to the time we have.

As busy professionals, we all know how challenging it can be to get home at a decent hour. For most of my clients, arriving home in time to have meals with family usually means speeding through traffic lights, taking calls on a cell phone while driving, and rushing in the door still fully focused on work issues.

We often forget in our attempt to spend quality time with the people we care about that there's just one thing these people want most: our full attention. After all, the people who walk in the door still stressed about work, yet patting themselves on the back for being there for their family are probably the same people who pace the sidelines of their children's sporting event while typing away on a smartphone or checking email. They're probably the same people who drill their family with questions about what they accomplished during the day, dish out critical feedback, eat as quickly as they race home, and then pass out on the couch in a food coma. Is that really *being there* for your family?

We've all experienced instances where we are physically present but completely absent mentally or emotionally (hopefully you're not doing that right now). We've also all had occasions when we didn't have much time available but managed to have an extraordinary experience because we were fully focused in the moment.

People with whom we have important relationships want nothing more from us than our attention—right here, right now. Practicing focusing exercises, such as those we discussed in Chapter 4 of this book, will help you train yourself to be more present for the people and things that matter most to you.

To increase your sense of connection, take a look at your current schedule. Try to identify times that you could either reach out to someone for a conversation or ask them to join you on a task or activity. This is a great opportunity for cross training, such as grabbing a friend or colleague to go for a walk so you can exercise while you connect. Or asking a family member to join you for a movie so you can improve your connection with them while getting some relaxation (if you chose the right movie, and the right family member, of course).

Lead by Example

One of the best ways to boost your accountability and commitment to this lifelong journey is to talk to other people about what you're doing, and teach them through your own example. My clients often ask me how to start discussions with their spouse or children about these concepts, and I always warn against preaching about healthy living. Even though they are passionate about improving their loved ones' health and longevity, having someone lecture you about all the things you already know you *should* be doing but haven't been able to do in the past is not helpful. In fact, the only thing it definitely *will* do is make them more stressed, and no doubt increase your stress levels at the same time.

By far, the best way to teach is by example. When *you* make the changes that you know are important, you show the people you care about the results, as you feel healthier, happier, more energized, more focused, and able to give them your full and best attention. Encourage them to participate with you by supporting your efforts. You just might find that in their effort to provide you accountability, they start making small shifts in their own behavior. This keeps stress and defense mechanisms down so that they don't interfere and make the situation worse.

SHARP Science: Help Your Child by Helping Yourself

A recent study published in the journal *Obesity* evaluated three types of parenting skills taught in family-based behavioral treatment for childhood obesity: (1) parenting style and techniques (such as limiting food consumption and encouraging physical activity), (2) changes in home food environment, and (3) parent modeling of weight-loss–supportive behaviors. Consistent with previously published research, parent BMI change was the only significant predictor of children's weight loss, leading researchers to suggest that overweight parents lose weight in order to help their children with weight management.[11]

First, focus on your own preparation to begin or continue your SHARP Solution program. Stock your kitchen with healthy, high-nutrient-value foods that are easy to prepare, while making the less healthy options more difficult to access (the trash is usually a great place for these if it doesn't stress you out too much). Create routines that help you to get more movement throughout the day, such as setting an alarm to go off every hour to prompt you to get up and walk for a few minutes, climb a couple flights of stairs, or do some simple exercises by your desk.

Make it a habit to do some sort of full-body movement during commercials and encourage your family to participate with you, making a game of it. Don't *tell* them what they should be doing; just do it and invite them to participate when they are willing. This keeps everybody's stress levels down while encouraging participation when others feel ready.

The more you encourage others and share what you're working on for your own sake, the more opportunities you'll find to teach what you know. There is nothing that provides more commitment than becoming a teacher and striving to authentically practice what you preach. I realized when I began teaching others about self-care that if I was going to stand up on stage or in front of a classroom, I had better be a living example of how to do that or no one would ever take me seriously. And although it's still a challenge every day, it's a challenge that I know I can face head on—one that I believe I have the tools to tackle. And that makes me stronger over time.

Set Yourself Up for Success

One of the difficulties with changing behavior is that it often takes a lot of energy just to get started. This dilemma is especially problematic when you're feeling lethargic to begin with. Yet, you've probably had the experience of feeling sluggish but pushing yourself to go for a walk or hit the gym and feeling much more energized within just a few minutes. One important strategy that will help make healthy choices a regular part of your life is to decrease what's called activation energy.

In physics, activation energy is the stimulus required to cause some sort of reaction; in human behavior, it's the energy we must expend in order to do something new. In his book, *The Happiness Advantage*, Shawn Achor talks about his experience with activation energy when he was trying to practice guitar more frequently.[12] In his description of what he calls the 20-Second Rule, Achor put the guitar closer to the couch and moved the television remote further away—about 20 seconds away, to be exact. "What I had done here, essentially, was put the desired behavior on the path of least resistance, so it actually took less energy for me to pick up and practice the guitar than to avoid it." He calls it the 20-Second Rule, "because lowering the barrier to change by just 20 seconds was all it took to help me form a new life habit."

Achor recently told me about a similar strategy he used to help create a more consistent exercise routine. "I moved my athletic shoes right next to my bed and slept in my gym clothes for 21 days, decreasing the activation energy to exercise in the morning long enough to create a life habit." He also mentioned that he was very clear as to what type of exercise he was going to do each day, and he had a specific plan for that day's workout routine. When you don't plan ahead, you give your brain time to come up with a million excuses as to why it's better not to exercise. And with all that time to contemplate, it's easy to talk your way out of it.

Here are a few suggestions for applying the 20-Second Rule to add more physical activity in your day:

1. Keep your home exercise equipment such as treadmills or weight benches where you will be most likely to use them instead of in a dark room in your house where they are often used as storage space or a hanger for laundry.

2. Put dumbbells or a resistance band next to the couch in your living room so that you don't have to make an effort to find them if you want to exercise while watching TV.

3. Pack a gym bag and take it with you to work so you have what you need to exercise during a break or before you head home.

Simply put, the goal here is to make it easier to make healthy choices so that your brain will be less likely to talk you out of it.

Sustainable behavior change is not something that occurs as a result of doing a 30- or 90-day program, nor is it something that you master after doing it for a year. Living a healthy, happy, and balanced life requires making a daily commitment to put in the time and energy, knowing that the return on that investment is great. The more we are able to invest in our own energy, the better we are able to give that energy to the people and things that matter most to us.

Training Tips:
- Isolation can be bad for your health.
- Social connection is based on perception.
- Cross-train with social activities that boost health.
- Lead by example.
- Set yourself up for success.

Training Techniques:
- Schedule lunch with a colleague at least once a week.
- Plan a social night out at least once a week.
- Start a consistent date-night routine with your spouse or a friend.
- Join a club or meet-up group.
- Sign up for a sports league.
- Take (or teach) a class.
- Volunteer at least once a month.
- Attend religious or spiritual gatherings.
- Go on a yoga or meditation retreat.
- Attend the theater or a concert with friends regularly.

Training Exercise #6: Teach

Without forcing the conversation on an unwilling participant, reach out to a few people and let them know what you're working on in this book. When you find someone who asks questions or seems interested, ask them for permission to spend some time walking through the 5 phases of *The SHARP Solution*. If you have several people, you might consider starting your own accountability group or inviting them to participate in a private virtual class with one of our certified instructors. If you'd like more information on starting a SHARP Solution accountability group or leading a workshop, contact us for more information and facilitator tools at info@synergyprograms.com.

7

The SHARP Solution Plan

Now that we've walked through the process of how to train your brain to improve your health, happiness, and performance, it's time to identify an action plan that will provide the structure you need to put these concepts to work. As we create your SHARP Solution plan, let's first recap the key strategies we explored, which are broken down into five phases:

Phase One: Balance Your Brain: Balance brain chemistry with focused breathing exercises and other relaxation techniques.

1. Just relax.

Phase Two: Engage Your Heart: Tap into the passions of your heart to boost motivation and engagement.

1. Recognize core values.
2. Establish purpose.
3. Create a vision statement.

Phase Three: Focus Your Mind: Shift out of multitasking mode into a more focused, mindful awareness of the present moment.

1. Increase awareness.
2. Master mindfulness.
3. Makeover your mindset.

Phase Four: Energize Your Body: Nourish your physical energy through strategic nutrition, physical activity, rest, and sleep.

1. Balance blood sugar.
2. Optimize blood flow.
3. Prioritize rest and sleep.

Phase Five: Strengthen Your Community: Build social support and accountability to help you stay consistent in the midst of daily challenges.

1. Establish social support.
2. Lead by example.
3. Set yourself up for success.

It can be helpful to first go through each phase and jot down the exercises and training tools that you think you might want to incorporate in the future. From there, you can narrow the list down to the primary action steps that you will implement right away. To help you with this process, I've put together some of the most common rituals that my clients have found helpful in the next section. Once you have them all down, go back and determine *one* key training exercise (or ritual) that you will incorporate for each dimension. This will allow you to break the five phases into five simple steps that you can take each day to create a healthier brain that operates most effectively and efficiently.

Make sure that the exercises you choose are not going to require so much energy that they cause your brain to resist. Remember, your brain is the conductor of your energy resources and its main job is to make sure you have what you need to survive, so excess spending is not desirable even if you *feel* like you really want to do the work. Start with the strategies that you feel are most important to you now and are also realistic to incorporate into your already busy schedule, and likely to lead to other positive changes.

1. **Balance Your Brain.** What key strategies will be important for you to consistently balance your brain chemistry?

   Sample exercises: Schedule two- to three-minute recharge breaks throughout the day; do full-body stretching;
   take a walk in nature; meditate (passive or active); explore
   relaxing visualization or guided imagery; practice deep-
   breathing exercises; laugh, play, have fun; take a yoga class;
   get a massage or other spa service; practice other stress
   management rituals that help bring brain chemistry back
   into balance by initiating the relaxation response.

2. **Engage Your Heart.** What key strategies will be important
   for you to consistently engage the passions of your heart?

   Sample strategies: Read your purpose statement out
   loud at key times throughout the day; place motivational
   statements or photographs in your environment and reflect
   on them regularly; subscribe to a blog, newsletter, or email
   that reminds you to think about your purpose (such as our
   SHARP Strategies group on LinkedIn); plan to call home
   at a certain time each day to connect with family; engage in
   spiritual practices such as prayer or reading scripture; read
   inspirational books or stories to start or finish the day; discuss the importance of purpose with family or friends; keep
   a daily journal recording times you felt on purpose or in the
   zone; create an inspirational ringtone that will remind you
   of your purpose each time you receive a phone call.

3. **Focus Your Mind.** What key strategies will be important
   for you to consistently quiet and focus your mind?

   Sample strategies: Schedule 50- or 55-minute "hours"
   so you have time in between appointments to relax, reflect,
   and prepare for your next meeting; do distraction resistance

and focusing exercises; practice visualization; utilize bio-feedback for controlling attention; play concentration games online (see www.synergyprograms.com/braingym for examples); complete challenge puzzles and brain teasers; schedule time for reflection and creativity regularly throughout the day; write down three things you're grateful for each morning; send a thank-you card to someone you appreciate each week.

4. **Energize Your Body.** What key strategies will be important for you to consistently fuel and energize your body?

Sample strategies: Eat something balanced every three to four hours; plan strategic snacks mid-morning and mid-afternoon; drink water consistently (fill a large jug or container each morning and set a goal to finish it before heading home at the end of the day); get out of your chair and move for at least five minutes every hour; lead a walking group at your office; train for a run or cycling event; go to bed earlier; plan a new bedtime ritual to help you fall asleep; avoid caffeine after noon; try to get seven to eight hours of sleep every night.

5. **Strengthen Your Community.** What key strategies will be important for you to consistently build and strengthen your community?

Sample strategies: Schedule lunch with a colleague at least once a week; plan a social night out at least once a week; start a consistent date-night routine; join a club or meet-up group; sign up for a sports league; take (or teach) a class; volunteer at least once a month; attend religious or spiritual gatherings; go on a yoga or meditation retreat; attend the theater or a concert with friends regularly.

As you think through your plan, be sure to incorporate the following SHARP guidelines as you chose your strategies:

Schedule – Decide *when specifically* you're going to practice each strategy and put it in your calendar as a priority.

Help – Think through helpful tools you can use for your practice, such as guided audio tracks, videos, and training software.

Accountability – Determine how you will hold yourself accountable each day. Some people find it useful to keep a training log or journal and check in regularly to track progress. Talk about what you're working on with others in order to provide extra accountability, and don't forget to celebrate small successes along the way!

Routine – Look for ways you can tie in new strategies with routines you have already built throughout the day, such as keeping your TV remote next to your running shoes or your vitamins next to your coffee pot.

Practice – Recognize that training will require consistent repetition in order to change the way your brain operates. Give yourself time and make sure you don't take on too many new strategies at once.

Now, select one new exercise or ritual that you feel you can realistically incorporate into your schedule for each of the five phases: balance your brain, engage your heart, focus your mind, energize your body, and strengthen your community. Create a training log or other list that lets you track your daily progress to help with accountability and consistency as you work to create new supportive habits. For a sample training log, visit www.synergyprograms.com/braingym.

Training for Success

I like to compare the brain to a muscle. While most of us are aware that it's use it or lose it when it comes to our physical fitness, it might seem like a stretch to many of you to train your brain like you do your body. Of course, a successful training program must find the right balance of being challenging enough to stimulate growth, but not causing so much discomfort that it breaks you down or makes you want to throw in the towel. To maximize your return on investment, consider the following training principles, which are based on physical fitness training guidelines:

New/Novel: In order for training to stimulate growth, it must require us to do something different. If we continue to do the same things over and over again, we just strengthen the same pathways without making progress. While stronger pathways are important when it comes to maintaining good habits, an exercise must cause us to adapt somehow if it's going to provide additional benefit. For example, someone who has done crossword puzzles might be able to do them without much thought. While this is great for relaxation and entertainment, it's not very helpful in stimulating new neural pathways in the brain to keep you sharp. Similarly, if you've been walking 30 minutes every day and you want to *increase* your physical energy it's important to do something new, whether it's walking hills instead of flat routes, speeding up, or adding a light jog every now and then.

Challenge: Training must push you out of your comfort zone a bit if it's going to be beneficial. Therefore, you want to make sure that anything you add to your routine is challenging and requires a bit of mental energy. If you find that you're having a difficult time consistently following your program, take a look at the exercises to make sure that none of them are causing your brain too much discomfort and putting you into "survival mode"—or what I like to call, "I'll do it tomorrow" mode.

Repetition: It's true that if you don't continue to use it, you *will* start to lose it! It's critical that we stay consistent with our practice in order for our training to have a lasting effect. If you've been a regular at the gym you know it only takes a few days, maybe a week at most, to start to feel like you're starting over again with your fitness routine. One or two days away might be good to restore energy, but more than that and your brain might start trying to talk you out of it once again. Remember, conserving energy seems like a better idea from a survival perspective—especially to a tired brain or one that's been out of practice for a while.

By incorporating challenging new rituals into your routine (without adding too much stress) and repeating them consistently, you can optimize your operating system and train your brain to change your body for the better.

As with all journeys in life, don't expect this to be a straight line from where you are now to where you want to go. Anticipating challenges and obstacles is an important part of planning for success. Before you begin, think through any situations or circumstances that you think might impede your program. Common challenges include travel, hosting company, entertaining clients, a busy social schedule, or a greater than normal workload. Looking ahead at your schedule on a regular basis will help you prepare alternative solutions so that you can keep moving forward—even if it's temporarily at a slower pace than you may like. Also, keep in mind that challenges and obstacles provide the best opportunity to learn; in fact, we experience what has been called *deep learning* when we make mistakes and have to fix them. On the one hand, we don't necessarily learn much along the way when it's smooth sailing. On the other hand, we are forced to focus more of our energy and attention on our immediate situation when we have to adjust our plan, leading us to make more of a lasting impression on our brain.

If at any time you find yourself at a standstill, go back through the process of aligning your CFO brain and CEO heart to make sure that you're able and willing to continue the journey. Make adjustments such as decreasing the number of exercises you're working on in order to relieve some of the energy burden during difficult times. This will keep your brain in a balanced state so that it can continue to support you on your journey. It's much better to be doing one or two energy enhancing exercises than to have a list of five that you never get to because it's too overwhelming. If at any point you find you would like assistance in the planning or execution of your plan, reach out to us at coach@synergyprograms.com for support!

Create Your Plan

Sample Plan
1. Balance My Brain.
   Daily recharge, three minutes three times a day at 11am, 2pm, and 5pm.

2. Engage My Heart.

    Write down my motivation for change each morning as #1 on my daily to-do list.

3. Focus My Mind.

    Do 20 minutes of meditation to quiet my mind at least once a day.

4. Energize My Body.

    Set a timer and move every 90 minutes.

5. Strengthen My Community.

    Meet with a friend at least once a week for a walk, coffee break, or lunch.

Motivation: More clarity of mind and creativity for writing.

My Plan

1. Balance My Brain.

_____

2. Engage My Heart.

_____

3. Focus My Mind.

_____

4. Energize My Body.

_____

5. Strengthen My Community.

_____

Motivation: _____

_____

Final Thoughts

It wasn't until I began to understand the magnitude of Alzheimer's disease that I realized we are neglecting our most valuable resource: our brainpower. The brain not only controls the day-to-day operations of the human system, it is home to our sense of self, our personality, and our soul. If you've experienced the devastation of seeing a loved one suffer from brain disease you are well aware of how quickly you can be robbed of the person you once knew. Kind, gentle, patient family members and friends seem to transform into irritated, angry, and sometimes mean strangers in a familiar looking body. Change the brain and you change the *being*—positively or negatively.

When you see how clearly we depend on our brains it seems obvious that we should be taking all possible measures to protect this critical asset. Yet our current lifestyle not only opens the door for brain disease and disorder, it actually fuels brain destruction! Too much stress and not enough recovery literally speeds up the deterioration process of our brain and our body. Eating processed foods and toxins, being sedentary, and losing our sense of connection with the world around us wears away at the structure of the brain, compromising our ability to function at our best.

As we continue to learn more about how the brain works we will continue to develop strategies for building a healthier, stronger, more resilient brain that supports us in accomplishing our missions in life. Perhaps the best news of all is that we don't have to wait to receive these benefits—training and maintaining our brain helps us look, feel, and perform better immediately; and the more we keep up our cognitive fitness routine, the better we will be able to live in the future. Train your brain to energize your life today, and protect and condition your brain to support a healthier, happier tomorrow!

Notes

Chapter 1 Understand Your Operating System

1. Nummenmaa, L., et al. (2012). Dorsal Striatum and Its Limbic Connectivity Mediate Abnormal Anticipatory Reward Processing in Obesity. *PLoS ONE*, 7(2): e31089. DOI: 10.1371/journal.pone.0031089.
2. Colzato., L., Ozturk, A., & Hommel, B., (2012). Meditation to Create: The Impact of Focused-Attention and Open-Monitoring Training on Convergent and Divergent Thinking. *Frontiers in Pscyhology*, 3. DOI: 10.3389/fpsyg.2012.00116.
3. Rissman, R., et al., (2012). Corticotrophin-releasing factor receptor-dependent effects of repeated stress on tau phophorylation, solubility, and aggregation. *Proceedings of the National Academy of Sciences*, DOI: 10.1073/pnas.1203140109.
4. University of Bergen, (May 7, 2012). Are you a Facebook addict? *ScienceDaily*. Retrieved June 19, 2012, from http://www.sciencedaily.com/releases/2012/05/120507102054.htm.
5. Medina, J., (2009). *Brain Rules*. Seattle, WA: Pear Press.
6. Jakubowicz, D., et al., (2011). Meal timing and composition influence in ghrelin levels, appetite scores and weight loss maintenance in overweight and obese adults. *Steroids*, DOI: 10.1016/j.steroids.2011.12.006.

7. Society for General Microbiology, (January 5, 2012). Couch potato or elite athlete? A happy medium keeps colds at bay. *ScienceDaily*. Retrieved June 19, 2012, from http://www.sciencedaily.com/releases/2012/01/120105112158.htm.

8. Sapolsky, R., (2004). *Why Zebras Don't Get Ulcers*. New York: Holt Paperbacks.

9. Luders, E., et al., (2012). The unique brain anatomy of meditation practitioners: Alterations in cortical gyrification. *Frontiers in Human Neuroscience*, DOI: 10.3389/fnhum.2012.00034.

10. Loehr, J., & Schwartz, T., (2003). *The Power of Full Engagement: Managing Energy, Not Time, Is the Key to High Performance and Personal Renewal*. New York, NY: Free Press.

Chapter 2 Balance Your Brain

1. Wallace Robert K, Benson Herbert, Wilson AF. A wakeful hypometabolic Physiologic state. *American Journal of Physiology* 1971;221:795–9.

2. Levy, D., et al., (May 2012). The effects of mindfulness meditation training on multitasking in a high-stress information environment. *Proceedings of Graphics Interface*.

3. Oh, H., & Taylor, A., (2011). Brisk walking reduces ad libitum snacking in regular chocolate eaters during a workplace simulation. *Appetite*, DOI: 10.1016/j.appet.2011.11.006.

4. Yuen, E., et al., (2012). Repeated stress causes cognitive impairment by suppressing glutamate receptor expression and function in prefrontal cortex. *Neuron*, DOI: 10.1016/j.neuron.2011.12.033.

5. Pascual-Leone A., (2001). The brain that plays music and is changed by it. *Annals New York Academy of Sciences*, 930, 315–329.

Chapter 3 Engage Your Heart

1. Buettner, D., (2008). *The Blue Zones: Lessons for Living Longer From the People Who've Lived the Longest*. Washington, DC: National Geographic Books.
2. Rush University Medical Center, (May 7, 2012). Greater purpose in life may protect against harmful changes in the brain associated with Alzheimer's Disease. *ScienceDaily*. Retrieved June 18, 2012, from http://www.sciencedaily.com /releases/2012/05/120507164326.htm.
3. University of Nebraska–Lincoln, (January 12, 2012). Imagine that: How you envision others says a lot about you in real life. *ScienceDaily*. Retrieved June 19, 2012, from http: //www.sciencedaily.com/releases/2012/01/120112193444 .htm.
4. Chang, S., et al., (2012). Inhaled oxytocin amplifies both vicarious reinforcement and self-reinforcement in rhesus macaques (Macaca mulatta). Proceedings of the National Academy of Sciences, DOI: 10.1073/pnas .1114621109.
5. Cousins, N., (2001). *Anatomy of an Illness as Perceived by the Patient: Reflections on Healing and Regeneration*. New York, NY: W. W. Norton & Company.

Chapter 4 Focus Your Mind

1. Asplund, C., Dux, P., Ivanoff, J., & Marois, R., (2006). Isolation of a central bottleneck of information processing with time-resolved fMRI. *Neuron*, 52(6), 1109–1120.

2. Reuters Business Information, (1996). *Dying for information? An investigation into the effects of information overload in the UK and worldwide.* London: Reuters Business Information.

3. American Academy of Pediatrics, (April 29, 2012). Driven to distraction: Anticipating cell phone calls may increase risk of a crash. *ScienceDaily*. Retrieved July 1, 2012, from http://www.sciencedaily.com/releases/2012/04/12042908 5408.htm Bottom of Form.

4. Gallagher, W., (2009). *Rapt: Attention and the Focused Life.* New York, NY: Penguin Press.

5. Wang, Z., & Tchernev, J., (2012). The "Myth" of Media Multitasking: Reciprocal Dynamics of Media Multitasking, Personal Needs, and Gratifications. *Journal of Communication*, DOI: 10.1111/j.1460-2466.2012.01641.x.

6. Speca, M., Carlson, L., Goodey, E., Angen, M., (2000). A randomized, wait-list controlled clinical trial: The effect of mindfulness meditation-based stress reduction program on mood and symptoms of stress in cancer patients. *Psychosomatic Medicine*, 62, 613–622.

7. Budzynski, T., (2011). Twilight Learning Revisited. *Biofeedback* 39(4): 155 DOI: 10.5298/1081-5937-39.4.08.

8. Levy, B., et al., (2002). Longevity increased by positive self-perceptions of aging. *Journal of Personality and Social Psychology*, 83(2), 261–270.

9. Marmot, M., Bosma, H., Hemingway, H., Brunner, E., & Stansfield, S., (1997). Contribution of job control and other

risk factors to social variations in coronary heart disease incidence. *The Lancet*, 350(9073), 235–240.

10. European Society of Cardiology (ESC), (August 28, 2011). Laughter has positive impact on vascular function. *ScienceDaily*. Retrieved June 19, 2012, from http://www.sciencedaily.com/releases/2011/08/110828101806.htm.

11. Crane, J.D., Ogborn, D.I., Cupido, C., Melov, S., Hubbard, A., Bourgeois, J.M., Tarnopolsky, M.A., (2012). Massage Therapy Attenuates Inflammatory Signaling After Exercise-Induced Muscle Damage. *Science Translational Medicine* 4(119): 119ra13 DOI: 10.1126/scitranslmed.3002882.

Chapter 5 Energize Your Body

1. Fernandez, A., & Goldberg, E., (2009). *The Guide to Brain Fitness: 18 interviews with scientists, practical advice, and product reviews, to keep your brain sharp*. Retrieved from http://www.sharpbrains.com/book/.

2. Talbot, K., et al., (2012). Demonstrated brain insulin resistance in Alzheimer's disease patients is associated with IGF-1 resistance, IRS-1 dysregulation, and cognitive decline. *Journal of Clinical Investigation*, DOI: 10.1172/JCI59903.

3. Agrawal, R., & Gomez-Pinilla, F., (2012). Metabolic syndrome in the brain: deficiency in omega-3 fatty acid exacerbates dysfunctions in insulin receptor signaling and cognition. *The Journal of Physiology* 590(10): 2485, DOI: 10.1113/jphysiol.2012.230078.

4. Scarmeas, N., et al., (August 2009). Physical Activity, Diet, and risk of Alzheimer disease. *JAMA*, 302(6), 627–37.

5. Miller, M., & Shukitt-Hale, B., (2012). Berry fruit enhances beneficial signaling in the brain. *Journal of Agricultural and Food Chemistry*. DOI: 10.1021/jf2036033.

6. Karnani, M., et al., (2011). Activation of central orexin/hypocretin neurons by dietary amino acids. *Neuron* 72(4): 616. DOI: 10.1016/j.neuron.2011.08.027.

7. Mayo Clinic, (May 1, 2012). Computer use and exercise combo may reduce the odds of having memory loss. *ScienceDaily*. Retrieved June 1, 2012, from http://www.sciencedaily.com/releases/2012/05/120501134201.htm.

8. Patel, A.V., Bernstein, L., Deka, A., Feigelson, H.S., Campbell, P.T., Gapstur, S.M., Colditz, G.A., & Thun, M. J., (2010). Leisure Time Spent Sitting in Relation to Total Mortality in a Prospective Cohort of US Adults. *American Journal of Epidemiology*, 172(4), 419–429.

9. Levine, J., et al., (2006). Non-Exercise Activity Thermogenesis: The Crouching Tiger Hidden Dragon of Societal Weight Gain. *Journal of Arteriosclerosis, Thrombosis, and Vascular Biology*, 2006 (26), 729–736.

10. B.C., Irwin, J., Scorniaenchi, N.L., Kerr, J.C., Eisenmann, D.L., Feltz, (2012). Aerobic Exercise Is Promoted when Individual Performance Affects the Group: A Test of the Kohler Motivation Gain Effect. *Annals of Behavioral Medicine*, DOI: 10.1007/s12160-012-9367-4.

11. National Institutes of Health, NIH Publication No. 06-5271 November 2005, Retrieved from http://www.nhlbi.nih.gov/health/public/sleep/yg_slp.htm.

12. Van Dongen, H., Rogers, N.L., & Dinges, D.F., (2003). Sleep debt: Theoretical and empirical issues. *Sleep and Biological Rhythms*, 1 (1), 5–13.

13. American Academy of Sleep Medicine (June 10, 2012). Brain scans show specific neuronal response to junk food when sleep-restricted. ScienceDaily. Retrieved June 19, 2012 from http://www.sciencedaily.com/releases/2012/06/120610151447.htm.

14. The Better Sleep Council, (2007). Position Statement: Poor sleep affects accuracy and attitude on the job. Retrieved from http://www.bettersleep.org.

15. Heffner, K, et al., (2012). Sleep disturbance and older adults' inflammatory responses to acute stress. American Journal of Geriatric Psychiatry, (1), DOI:10.1097/JPG.0b013e31824361de.

16. Van Dongen, H., Rogers, N., & Dinges, D., (2003). Sleep debt: Theoretical and empirical issues. Sleep and Biological Rhythms, 1(1), 5–13.

17. American Academy of Sleep Medicine (June 10, 2012). Brain scans show specific neuronal response to junk food when sleep-restricted. ScienceDaily. Retrieved June 19, 2012 from http://www.sciencedaily.com/releases/2012/06/120610151447.htm.

Chapter 6 Strengthen Your Community

1. Holt-Lunstad J., Smith T., & Layton J., (2010). Social Relationships and Mortality Risk: A Meta-analytic Review. *PloS Med*, 7(7), 1–20.

2. Cacioppo, J. & Patrick, W., (2008). *Loneliness: Human Nature and the Need for Social Connection*. New York, NY: W.W. Norton & Company.

3. Ibid.

4. Ybarra, O., Bernstein, E., Winkielman, P., Keller, M., Manis, M., Chan, E., & Rodriguez, J., (2008). Mental Exercising Through Simple Socializing: Social Interaction Promotes General Cognitive Functioning. *PSPB*, 34 (2), 248–259.

5. Hawkley, L, Masi, C., Berry, J., & Cacioppo, J., (2006). Loneliness is a unique predictor of age-related differences in systolic blood pressure. *Psychology and Aging*, 21(1), 152–164.

6. Perissinotto, C., Cenzer, I., & Covinsky, K., (2012). Loneliness in older persons: A predictor of functional decline and death. *Archives of Internal Medicine*, DOI: 10.1001/archinternmed.2012.1993.

7. Berkman, L., Leo-Summers, L., & Horwitz, R., (1992). Emotional Support and Survival after Myocardial Infarction: A Prospective, Population-based Study of the Elderly. *Ann.Intern Med*, 117(12), 1003–1009.

8. Bloom, J., (2001). Sources of support and the physical and mental well-being of young women with breast cancer. *Social Science & Medicine*, 53(11), 1513–1524.

9. Schnall, H. & Stefanucci, P., (2008). Social support and the perception of geographical slant. *Journal of Experimental Social Psychology*, 44, 1246–1255, DOI: 10.1016/j.jesp.2008.04.011.

10. Adams, R., Santo, J., & Bukowski, W., (2011). The presence of a best friend buffers the effects of negative experiences. *Developmental Psychology*, 47(6): 1786, DOI: 10.1037/a0025401.

11. Boutelle, K., Cafrie, G., & Crow, S., (2012). Parent predictors of child weight change in family-based behavioral obesity treatment. *Obesity*, DOI: 10.1038/oby.2012.48.

12. Achor, S., (2010). *The Happiness Advantage*. New York: Random House.

For More Information

Websites

For free brain training exercises and guided relaxation audio tracks, visit www.synergyprograms.com/braingym.

For meal planning ideas, including recipes, shopping strategies, and tips for eating on the go, visit www.synergyprograms .com/thesharpdiet.

Books

Brain Plasticity and Brain Training

Brain Rules, John Medina

Buddha's Brain, Rick Hanson

Imagine, Jonah Lehrer

Mindset, Carol Dweck

Mindsight, Daniel Siegel

Positivity, Barbara Fredrickson

Rapt, Winifred Gallagher

The Happiness Advantage, Shawn Achor

The How of Happiness, Sonja Lyubomirsky

The Talent Code, Daniel Coyle
Think Smart, Richard Restak
Willpower, Roy Baumeister and John Tierney

Healthy Aging
Counterclockwise, Ellen Langer
Flourish, Martin Seligman
The Blue Zones, Dan Buettner
Younger Next Year, Chris Crowley and Henry Lodge

Nutrition
Eat to Live, Joel Fuhrman
In Defense of Food, Michael Pollan
Mindless Eating, Brian Wansink
The Beck Diet Solution, Judith Beck
The End of Overeating, David Kessler

Physical Activity and Exercise
SPARK: The Revolutionary New Science of Exercise and the Brain, John Ratey

Stress Management
Getting Things Done, David Allen
The Relaxation Response, Herbert Benson
Why Zebras Don't Get Ulcers, Robert Sapolsky

Sleep
Power Sleep, James Maas

Social Connection
Loneliness, John Cacioppo & William Patrick

Purpose and Storytelling
Believe Me, Michael Margolis
The Power of Full Engagement, Jim Loehr and Tony Schwartz
The Power of Purpose, Richard Leider
The Power of Story, Jim Loehr

Index

A

Accountability, boosting, 153–155
Achor, Shawn, 155–156
Activation energy, 155
Addiction, 16, 17–18
Adrenaline, 104
Aging, books on, 182
American Institute of Stress, 24
American Journal of Epidemiology, 130
American Journal of Physiology, 42
Anatomy of an Illness (Cousins), 82–83
Anticipation, attention and, 92–93
Appetite (Journal), 51
Attention:
    anticipation and, 92–93
    focus of, 10, 11–12
    paying, concept of, 92
Attitude:
    non-judgmental, 59–60
    passive, 43
Audio aids, 59
Automated system (auto-brain), 25–27, 29, 31–32

B

Behavior:
    changing, difficulties of, 155
    controlling, 71
    loneliness and, 147–148
Benson, Herbert, 42, 43
Berntson, Gary, 146
Berries, brain and, 120
Better Sleep Council, 134
Biofeedback, 97–98, 106–107
Biofeedback (Journal), 98
Blood flow, optimizing, 127–132
Blood sugar, balancing, 117–120

The Blue Zones (Buettner), 70
Body energizing:
    balancing blood sugar, 117–120
    energy management techniques, 116
    exercise and, 116, 128
    optimizing blood flow, 127–133
    plan, prepare, and pack method, 125–127
    rest and recovery prioritization, 133–135
    return on investment maximization, 120–125
    in *SHARP Solution* plan, 161–162, 164
    sleep and, 135–139
    training and, 128, 140–141
Brain. *See also* Brain balancing; Brain training program; Lizard brain; Monkey brain
    berries and, 120
    boosting the power of, 25–27
    change and, 7–9, 33–34
    chemistry balancing of, 36–37
    cross-training, 105–107
    drain of, 118
    energized, 110
    as leader of human operating system, 3–8
    sharp, keeping, 12–13
    stress and, 11, 12, 15
    training of, 10–11, 103, 128, 181
Brain balancing:
    pausing and relaxing, 54–63
    recharging, 44–49
    relaxation response technique, 41, 42–44
    SHARP brain recharge process, 7, 49–54, 55

Brain balancing: (*Continued*)
  in *SHARP Solution* plan, 161, 163
  training and, 51–52, 63–65
Brain plasticity and brain training, books
    on, 181–182
Brain Resource, 106
Brain Rules (Medina), 19
Brain-training program:
  building, 34–37
  single-focus concept and, 29
Brainwashing, 98
Break taking:
  circulation and, 89
  to control carvings, 50–51
  maintaining memory by, 53
Breath counting, 58
Breathing exercise, 36–37, 55
Buettner, Dan, 70
Busyness, productivity and, 18

C
Caloric expenditure, 130
Cannon, Walter B., 42
Cacioppo, John, 146–147
Cell Phone Overuse Scale (CPOS), 92
Challenges:
  preparing for, 125–127
  of professionals, 151–152
Change:
  brain and, 7–9, 33–34
  stress as stimulus for, 13–15
Chunking strategy, 94
Cognitive fitness, 9, 47
Cognitive training, 34
Commitment, boosting, 153–155
Community, strengthening, 145–158,
    162, 164–165
Conservation, mental energy and, 88
Cortisol, 21, 24, 104
Cousins, Norman, 82
CPOS. *See* Cell Phone Overuse Scale
    (CPOS)
Cravings, controlling, 50–51
C-reactive protein (CRP), 133
Creative thinking, 10

Creativity:
  cultivating, 108–112
  stressed-out brain and, 11
CRP. *See* C-reactive protein (CRP)

D
Decision making:
  energy and, 5
  multitasking and, 27–28
Developmental Psychology (Journal), 151
Diet, 20, 125–127
Dopamine, 16

E
Efficiency, stressed-out brain and, 11
Endurance:
  brain and, 11, 48
  performance and, 12
Energy:
  mental, 35, 48, 93
  mental, managing, 87–89
  physical and heart, 35
  as valuable resource, 3–9,
    20–21
Energy investment strategy, 7
Entrepreneurs, barriers for, 4
Environment, quiet, 56–57
Exercise. *See also* Physical activity
  biofeedback, 106–107
  books on, 182
  breathing, 36–37, 55
  as energy investment strategy, 7
  forced, effects of, 23
  purposeful, 127–132
  rest and, 10

F
Facebook, 17–18, 150
Fernandez, Alvaro, 117
Fitness, vision of, 9–13
Flexibility:
  brain and, 11, 47
  mental, 10
  performance and, 12
Focused attention training, 10

Focus/focusing:
    of attention, 10, 11–12
    audio aids for, 59
    mental, 57–58, 95, 98–99
    on present moment, 93
    statement, 58–59
    visual aids for, 59
Food, 124, 125–127

G
Gallagher, Winifred, 95
Gleeson, Mike, 23
Goals:
    purpose and, 69–70
    reaching, 71
    of relaxation strategies, 46–49
Goldberg, Elkhonon, 117
Gratitude, building, 112

H
Habits, 32, 33–34
Happiness Advantage (Achor), 155
Harms, Peter, 78
Health:
    social connection and, 147, 148, 149
    stress and, 19–25
Heart engagement:
    achieving goals and, 69–70
    creating vision and, 71–72
    energy of, 35
    as leader in human operating system,
        3–9
    purpose statement and, 72–76
    in SHARP Solution plan, 161, 163
    telling your story, 76–80
    training and, 80–84
Heart rate variability (HRV), 106–107
HRV. See Heart rate variability (HRV)
Human mortality, stress and, 13
Human operating system:
    improving habits, 33–34
    leaders overseeing, 3–9
    multitasking and, 27–32
    new vision of fitness, 9–13
    relaxing the body and mind and, 15–19

stress and, 13–15, 19–25
training plan, 24–37

I
Ideas, 10
Ikigai concept, 70
Interpersonal empathy mode, mind and,
    11
Investing strategically, mental energy
    and, 89

J
James, William, 103
Journal of Agricultural and Food Chemistry,
    120
Journal of Social Psychology, 102
Just, Marcel, 92

K
Kabat-Zinn, John, 96

L
LaLanne, Jack, 127
Laughter, 82–84, 108
Leadership, success and, 69
Leading by example, 153–155
Lizard brain, 26, 27, 29
Locus of control, 105
Loehr, Jim, 32
Loneliness:
    behavior and, 147–148
    negative consequences of, 149
    perception and, 149–150
Loneliness: Human Nature and the Need for
    Social Connection (Cacioppo and
    Patrick), 146

M
Massage:
    inflammation reduction and, 110
    stress and, 108–109
MBSR. See Mindfulness-Based Stress
    Reduction (MBSR)
Meal planning and recipes, website on,
    181

Medina, John, 19
Meditation:
  mental muscle and, 30
  mindfulness and, 97
  mindsight and, 100–101
  multitasking and, 45–46
  open monitoring, 10
  relaxation programs and, 54
Mediterranean diet, 119
Memory maintenance, taking breaks to, 53
Mental energy, 35, 48, 87–89, 93
Mental fitness, 11, 12
Mental flexibility, 10
Mental focusing, 57–58, 95, 98–99
Mental stress, 11
Mind focusing:
  brain cross-training, 105–108
  cultivating creativity, 108–111
  managing mental energy, 87–89
  mindfulness and, 95–98
  mindset makeover, 101–105
  multitasking and monkey brain, 89–94
  SHARP Solution plan, 161, 163–164
  training and, 111–112
  turning mindfulness into mindsight, 98–101
Mindfulness
  importance of, 95–98
  turning into mindsight, 98–101
Mindfulness-Based Stress Reduction (MBSR), 46, 96–97
Mindset, optimistic, creating, 101–105, 112
Mindsight:
  meditation, 100–101
  turning mindfulness into, 98–101
Monkey brain, 26, 28, 89–94
Monkey love, 81–82
Multi-prioritizing, 88
Multitasking
  avoiding, 27–32, 88, 94
  meditation and, 45–46
  monkey brain and, 89–94
  as necessary skill, 95–96
My Calm Beat, 106

N
National Institute on Aging, 148
National Institutes of Health, 134
National Sleep Foundation, 133, 139
NEAT. *See* Non-exercise activity thermogenesis (NEAT)
Neural nutrients, 123
Non-exercise activity thermogenesis (NEAT), 130–131, 140–141
Non-judgmental attitude, 59–60
Nutrients, neural, 123
Nutrition:
  books on, 182
  well-being and, 9

O
Obesity, the brain and, 6
Obesity (Journal), 153
Open monitoring meditation, 10
Oscillation, 10

P
Parasympathetic nervous system, 41
Parenting skills, 153–154
Pascual-Leone, Alvaro, 61
Passive attitude, 43
Patrick, William, 146
Perception:
  connection and, 149–150
  stories and shape of, 77–78
Performance:
  multitasking and, 28
  stress and, 12–13
Personal energy, 3, 22
Personal engagement, 69
PFC. *See* Pre-frontal cortex (PFC)
Physical activity, 132
  books on, 182
  well-being and, 9
Physical energy, 35
Physical fitness, 9, 11
Positive mindset, 101–105

Posture, comfortable, 57
The Power of Full Engagement
   (Loehr and Schwartz), 32
Pre-frontal cortex (PFC), 53
Problem solving, 106–107
Purpose:
   books on, 183
   goals and, 69–70
   sense of, 73, 148–149
   statement, 72–76

R
Rapt (Gallagher), 95
Rebalancing, as goal of relaxation
   strategy, 47
Recharging:
   as goal of relaxation strategy, 48–49
   SHARP brain recharge process, 49–54
   tools and strategies, 62
Recovery:
   as goal of relaxation strategy, 46–47
   mode, mind and, 11
   prioritizing, 133–135
   social support and, 148
   well-being and, 9
Reflective system (thinking brain),
   25–27
Relationships, building, 151–152
Relaxation:
   as hard work, 15–19
   meditation and, 54–55
   pause and, 54–62
   strategies, utilizing, 46–49
   stress and, 137–138
   techniques of, 10
Relaxation response, 41, 42–44
Resources, human operating system and,
   3–9
Rest:
   exercise and, 10
   periodic, 11
   prioritizing, 133–135
   well-being and, 9
Resting metabolic rate (RMR), 130
Rest mode, shifting to, 11

Return on investment (ROI),
   maximizing, 120–125
RMR. *See* Resting metabolic rate (RMR)

S
Safety, brain and, 35
Sapolsky, Robert, 24
Scheduling, 56
Schwartz, Tony, 32
Selye, Hans, 13
Sense of purpose, connection and, 73,
   148–149
SHARP Brain recharge process, 49–54,
   55
The Sharp Brains Guide to Brain Fitness
   (Fernandez and Elkhonon), 117
SHARP Solution Plan
   brain balancing, 161, 163
   community strengthening, 162,
   164–165
   creating, 168–169
   energizing the body, 161–162, 164
   focusing the mind, 161, 163–164
   heart engagement, 161, 163
Siegel, Dan, 99
Single-focus concept, brain-training
   program and, 29
Sleep:
   amount of, 135–137
   books on, 182
   lack of, 133–135
   oscillation and, 137–141
   strategies of, 138–141
Snacks, balanced, 124
Social connection:
   basis and lack of, 145–146
   books on, 182
   perception and, 149–150
Social networking websites, 150
Social neuroscience, 146
Social support, 147–148
Spending wisely, mental energy and,
   87–88
Storytelling, books on, 183
Strategy, chunking, 94

Strength:
    brain and, 11, 47
    performance and, 12
Stress:
    addiction and, 16–18
    books on management of, 182
    cognitive health and, 13
    creativity and, 11
    excess fat storage and, 104
    health and, 19–25
    human system and, 13–15
    massage and, 108–109
    mental, 11
    relaxation and, 137–138
Stress response, 41
Success:
    leadership and, 69
    setting up for, 155–157
    training for, 166–168
Support building:
    connection and perception, 149–150
    leading by example, 153–155
    quantity *vs.* quality, 150–151
    relationships and, 151–152
    setting up for success, 155–158
    social connection, 145–149
Survival mode, energy shortage and, 3

T
Teams, exercising with, 132
Thinking, 10, 106–107
Time management, 94
Tools and strategies, recharge, 62
Training techniques/tips:
    to balance the brain, 63
    to energize the body, 140
    on engage the heart, 80–81, 81

    to live healthy, happy, and balanced
        life, 157
    to shifting mind focus, 111–112
Training/training exercises:
    of the brain, 9, 10–11, 51–52, 63–65
    breathing, 36–37
    on building gratitude, 112
    focused attention, 10
    habit and, 33–34
    heart engagement and, 80–84
    mind focusing and, 111–112
    NEAT day, 140–141
    plan, 34–35
    success and, 166–168
    teaching people, 158
20-Second Rule, 155–156

V
Values, wellness and, 75
Vision:
    creating clear, 71–72
    of fitness, 9–13
Visual aids, for focusing, 59
Visualization, 60–62

W
Websites, 72, 111, 181
Well-being, cognitive fitness and, 9
Wellness:
    programs, 9
    values and, 74–75
Why Zebras Don't Get Ulcers (Sapolsky),
        24

Y
Yan, Zhen, 53
Ybarra, Oscar, 147